You Can Bet the Ranch

You
Can Bet
the Ranch

by

Pat Wellman

Beacon Hill Press of Kansas City
Kansas City, Missouri

ISBN: 083-411-1551

Printed in the
United States of America

Cover: Crandall Vail

Permission to quote from the following copyrighted version is acknowledged with appreciation:
The Holy Bible, New International Version (NIV), copyright © 1973, 1978,
    1984 by the International Bible Society.

10   9   8   7   6   5   4   3   2   1

To our four wonderful children:
Wally and Debbie,
Steve and Sue.
Two of them
are in-laws,
but love has erased
the distinction!

Contents

Preface

I couldn't afford Harris or Gallup, so I conducted my own survey. Just as I suspected, about half those polled knew the expression "You can bet the ranch!" I suspected, too, that those who were familiar with it were Midwesterners. That, also, proved to be true. That's because it is a Midwestern idiom for "This is a sure thing. Stake your life on it!" I suppose the coastal population, east or west, would prefer "You can bet your bottom dollar!"

As for betting, well, that's a horse of a different color. The Christian community (most assuredly the Midwesterners) would not consider that appropriate. Me, either, for I don't believe in gambling in any form. So I talked to the Lord about this title.

"Lord, I want to use it, and it really is a matter of speech and not an admonition. I only want to remind the whole world that YOU can be counted on when nothing else can be!"

"Use it," He OK'd. "Just be sure to explain it!"
I just did.

Love from a Midwesterner,
PAT

Introduction

My eyes wandered slowly around the beautiful sanctuary. Everywhere, candles blinked a warm hello. That was a fulfillment of a wish on Sue's priority list. "When I get married," she had said at a very early age, "I want lots and lots of candles." And here they were—lots of them. So many that they by themselves, I thought, could sufficiently light the way for the bride.

The flowers that so effectively completed the panorama of beauty were our favorites. Each blossom appeared to have been put in its place with a great deal of love, reflecting a long, close relationship with our friend the florist. It occurred to me that God, because of His great love, had painstakingly designed and placed each petal in its place, too, conveying to us a sense of peace and order. The world was at peace and in place.

I felt at peace, too. I knew that was a gift of God. Many times I had witnessed weddings at which, for various reasons, Mother was not at peace. Regardless, mothers are supposed to cry, it seemed. But I had no tears. Wally, our son, was one who expected some. Several times prior to the wedding he had asked, "Are you all right, Mom?" "Sure," I had replied with great composure. His concern was touching; no reason for him to know that just a few days before, I had cried for hours!

Until this moment the organ had softly blended the aura of candles and flowers with romantic music beautifully played and sung. Now, both piano and organ broke forth with great volume, signaling the climax of the processional. As the mother of the bride, I led the guests to their feet and turned to watch as Cinderella approached wearing both slippers!

I looked at Don—that old softy! In spite of his continual philosophical approach to this event, he was crying. That wasn't surprising. I knew he would. Fathers are not altogether unpredictable. I laughed to myself, remembering the day over a year ago when Sue and I took him to the department store for his first glimpse of the dress she was now wearing. On that day, she barely had time to emerge from the dressing room and straighten the folds of fabric in the full skirt before Dad suddenly knew he was needed at his office. He disappeared. It wasn't surprising then, either, to find him a few minutes later with tears trickling down his cheeks. He had forgotten we had come in the same car!

Just to my right stood Prince Charming. Steve was really that! Not only had God been good enough to send a son-in-law who possessed the exact strengths we had prayed for for our daughter, but He had made him very good-looking too. Steve was a strong young man, both physically and spiritually. He had been raised in an environment quite like Sue's, with identical religious beliefs and values. His parents, Bill and Robbie, were very special to us, and I thanked the Lord for them as I glanced beyond Steve to see their proud faces.

"Dearly beloved . . ."

I looked around thoroughly. Bridesmaids and groomsmen stood stationed at small intervals across the platform as if building a fence around their friends. Nothing but "beloved" shall intrude. They needn't worry, I thought; these two are *so* in love! They each have found their beloved, and their eyes light up, their smiles are personal and telling, and their dreams are of white knights and fairy princesses! Ah, what a romantic I am. How have I made it through reality all these years? Speaking of reality, my eyes stopped at Wally's face. He was crying!

"Do you take this man . . . this woman . . ."

I have never understood the need for this part of the ceremony. Why in the world would they be here if they did not intend to take each other? Do you suppose anyone has ever said, "No, I don't!" I laughed to myself. I envisioned a befuddled, don't-know-what-to-do-now minister swallowing his boutonniere!

"Let us pray . . ."

"Lord, we made it! You know how many times I have talked to You about this moment. Thank You for making it an exciting dream come true. Thank You for making these two perfect for each other. The four of us, in other places, brought them as babies to Your altar. Thank You for the continued reassurance that you were holding them in Your hand! We have encouraged them to be comfortable at Your altar at all times, and we are grateful that, as a result, they come to this one with confidence. They are learning to rely on You, Lord. Lead them from here!"

"I now pronounce you man and wife . . ."

Well, there they go: joy and happiness clothed in a tuxedo and flowing lace! The long aisle of the church stretches before them, and they will walk it together. It will lead them to the outstretched arms of a new life as one. Days shall become months, months shall evolve into years, and the years will add up to eternity. *They have it made!* Yessirree, I would "bet the ranch" on this marriage!

*   *   *

How fortunate that God had not given us a ranch!

Two years and two months later I found myself staring for the umpteenth time at the four walls of our bedroom. Steve and Sue had separated. The questions came so fast and were so varied it was hard to sort them out to *ask* them intelligently, much less *answer* them. By now God was probably tired of hearing my ramblings, too. Even on those occasions over the last two months when I had managed to make sense, He hadn't . . . made sense . . . or heard, it seemed.

The most obvious and oft-asked question was: What went wrong? Then came, How did we fail? How could all of us have been so wrong? Why was I so blind that it took me months to see what was happening? Could I have been so insensitive? What happened to all those years of training up a child, of planting the seeds of trust, faith, and love? Surely the world knew that separation and divorce were not supposed to occur in devout, dedicated ministers' families. That suggestion had been made often over the years, and I had laughed the laugh of the preposterous and smugly intellectualized that there was no segment of society immune to these things. That, of course, was before *my* heart and emotions had been invaded!

I have lived very few days as burdened and brokenhearted as that Saturday. Somehow my weary, numb body walked through the necessary chores of the day. Instinct, apparently. For years I had done the things that had to be done before the Sabbath. At a very late hour I followed my legs into the bathroom to take a bath, thereby finishing the list.

Now, I'm sure that all Christians have experienced special moments of intimate spiritual revelation—confrontation with spiritual truth—so intensely real and so definitely God-given that neither the intellect nor the will resists its impact. Several of those insights had already been framed and hung on the walls of my mind. But I hardly expected such an encounter while testing the temperature of the bathwater. Yet, there it was!

The rushing water jolted my preoccupation with the oppression of the day and the regret of totally lost hours. All of a sudden I started laughing! Not smiling, laughing! All semblance of heartache and depression disappeared, and I felt an indescribable peace!

The Lord himself was so close I actually spoke out loud to Him!

"How strange!"

Then came the thoughts. How can I be laughing? How is it that my spirit feels as though it has been resting all day? How can I possibly feel such peace?

Never shall I forget His next words. He spoke to me in my spirit, but nothing has ever been more audible.

"And the peace of God, which passeth all understanding, shall keep your hearts and minds through Christ Jesus" (Phil. 4:7).

Now, I had heard that verse of scripture all my life and had loved it just as long. It had a nice ring to it. But it never had been *real* until that moment. Since becoming a Christian, I had never really been in a position of need so great that having inner peace was totally unthinkable! The hurt had never been extreme enough to cancel understanding!

Again I questioned the Lord. "How is it possible that I can have a peace that transcends the anguish of this horrible day?"

He called me by name: "Pat, all the world suffers the consequences of Satan's deceit and destruction. The peace you have is the distinguishing difference between the struggle of the Christian and the battle of the unredeemed!"

14

A grand prix! The realization that when the human mind has reached and groped and searched, yet found no morsel of comprehension or scrap of wisdom to satisfy reason, the child of God is sustained by a peace that stretches past the waves of confusion and doubt and brings him to a harbor *infinitely safer than any offered by understanding alone!*

I will never forget that experience. It will stay with me as a bulwark forever. Furthermore, as I lived through the trying days that followed, I learned a companion lesson: There is nothing more attractive to the unbeliever than Christian peace. Oh, yes, the glowing verbal testimony of God's saving grace is important; the use of His Word to proclaim His love and goodness is impressive; and the admonition to embrace His salvation so freely given is necessary; but *nothing* speaks quite as loudly as the ability to exhibit His peace while riding out the storm! Peace that is genuine cannot be argued with.

Thus I began a new search—an exciting one. It led me to the words of Jesus. He said, "Peace I leave with you, my peace I give unto you" (John 14:27). How strange—Jesus was not a man of peace. The Bible distinctly declares Him a man of sorrows; He bore our griefs; He cried over Jerusalem with an immeasurable depth of sorrow; He lived His life knowing that death not only was imminent but also would be unjust and excruciating.

Yet, somehow and somewhere, He possessed and maintained in the deepest recesses of His nature a peace that no one fully understood. He boldly and lovingly offers a peace that is uniquely His. The apostle Paul was one of the first to comprehend. He rejoiced in Ephesians that Christ himself "is our peace" (2:14).

What is the source of the peace of our Savior? What ingredients constitute a peace that cannot be destroyed by a mad, dishonest, chaotic world? How is it safeguarded? Is there a correlation between the Redeemer's peace and His relation to His Father? Is the Holy Spirit involved in its perpetuation? Is it for ME?

May I share with you my discoveries? They are not new, but I pray earnestly that the results of my search will open some doors of confidence and assurance heretofore unrealized. So much of life is uncertain and unbelievable —but not these truths. In fact, you need not hesitate: "You can bet the ranch" on them!

1

Jesus Was Never Conquered by Stress

The Bible declares that Jesus experienced all of life. Therefore, He knew about stress. The mere scope of His activity would make it difficult to believe otherwise. The constant press and need of the crowd plus the enormity of His responsibility would have done most of us in. But He was the Master of all circumstance and was never conquered by stress.

Stress! What imagery and trauma is prompted by that word. Somewhere between birth and death we must learn to deal with stress.

Medical science tells us that mental health walks a fine line between sanity and insanity; psychology proclaims a very close kinship between love and hate; and neurology points out that the difference between coping and suicide or breakdown may be only a crisis away.

A most serious realization is that all of these functions are so closely related. The mind and emotions affect the nervous system to such great extent as to sometimes cause the breakdown of reasoning and/or psychical balance. It is astonishing to us who are not trained medically to witness the devastation experienced by the body as a result of mental and emotional distress. And it is almost inconceivable to most of us that each year more than 70 million prescriptions are issued for tranquilizers in an attempt to combat and control these interactions. Taking pills is a national pastime!

Don and I were chatting over breakfast coffee when the morning news suddenly captured our attention. Dr. Tim Johnson, a regular commentator on ABC's "Good Morning, America," made a startling statement: "We now know that 50 to 80 percent of all illnesses are caused by stress."

I started calculating. There are a lot of illnesses that were definitely stress-oriented. I was not far removed from the day I stood in an I.C.U. cubicle watching my brother find consciousness again following a five-artery bypass surgery.

"Stress," his doctor had explained, "has a great deal to do with heart problems." He described stress as a "social" disease.

I remembered chatting with the nurse.

"Do women have bypass surgery?" Up to that time I had not known any who had.

"Yes," she replied, "more and more!"

As women assume those jobs traditionally held by men, they also are becoming victims of those illnesses usually associated with males. That is not to say that any one ailment has ever been exclusively related to one sex or the other. But "equal opportunity" illness has tagged along with "equal opportunity" employment and life-style. Certain occupations come equipped with reservoirs of stress.

But wait just a minute. The obvious does not add up to 50 to 80 percent! I began the enumerating of some things I felt *could not* be caused by stress. It was a long list. However, hardly a week had gone by when a dear friend called to say she was very disturbed: She had discovered several lumps in her breasts. (That was on my not-caused-by-stress list.) Little did I know. After extensive examination and testing we were both amazed and very relieved to be told by her physician that the lumps were the result of the tremendous stress she had been experiencing at her job!

Shortly after that, I was scanning the current issue of a leading magazine. An article listing the ramifications of stress caught my eyes. The writer must have seen my list! She almost demolished it. Besides heart disease, cancer, diabetes, accidental injuries, and cirrhosis of the liver, she included lower-back pain and skin problems as often being caused by stress. It was surprising to know that stress actually decreases our immunity to several kinds of infections.

I believe with all my heart that since Christ was not conquered by stress, He would not have us be either. We should apply ourselves to understanding what it is that brings stress into our lives, and make deliberate efforts to deal knowledgeably with stressful situations and periods of energy-sapping frustration.

Like a piece of elastic, each of us has some "give" in us. But what are the sources of pressure that bring us either to the limits of the "give" or render us rigid and unbending? Can our resiliency be measured like the stress factor, for instance, of a piece of steel?

Some of the causes are obvious because they are so general. For instance, one of the most successful culprits is change: changing morals (in and out of the church), a very mobile populace, the precarious national and personal financial structures, the changing status of relationships, and, yes, just *change*, period!

Sure, change is as old as the Colorado mountains I can see outside my window. In fact, it has been reported that as Adam and Eve left the garden, Eve was heard saying, "Adam, I think we are in a period of transition!" The *new* about change is that it is now a life-style. For some it becomes that at a very early age.

I should be ashamed, I know, but usually I do not care to sit with children on an airplane—that is, children who are traveling alone. Many times I've been happy to help a mother with small children, but for some reason when a child is alone the mother in me feels responsible. And children are unpredictable. I never know if they will sit up, stand up, act up, or throw up!

On a recent trip the third seat in our row was taken by a small girl dressed in blonde hair, blue eyes, and a California tan that spoke of hours in the sun. Promptly she went to sleep. Good, I thought. However, she woke up shortly, and I soon realized that her tiny nap was only fortification for the nonstop chattering that followed.

She was seven years old, was on her way from California to Ohio to see her father, and would change planes in Denver. She spoke excitedly about the corn on the cob, Twinkies, and popcorn she would have with her daddy. She *said* she spent a year in California and a year in Ohio, but I doubt she understood time periods that clearly.

"Did your mommy tell you not to talk to strangers?" I asked.

"Oh, no," she said as she patted my arm, "it's OK. I like people. When I grow up I am going to do something to help people. I will either be a cab driver or a doctor!"

I laughed in spite of her intense sincerity.

She was full of information about her family, although I lost out somewhere along the line as to who was where and who belonged to whom. I did conclude that in California there was definitely a home consisting of yours, mine, and ours. In Ohio, so far, there was just yours and mine, although Daddy was going to marry, and there might be ours! The seven-year-old seemed to understand it.

Sensing we were nearing our descent into Denver, she reached for her possessions and took out her ticket and related papers.

"You sure are a big girl," I bragged, "taking care of your own ticket and belongings and even changing planes!"

Suddenly my 7-year-old friend was 20! She sat up straight as if to meet me as an equal. Her eyes aimed at mine like the hunter's bead on a bird. She squared her jaw.

"*I'm* a big girl *for changing people all the time!*" she said.

And with a bitter whisper, as if not wanting me to hear, she added, "I hate going back and forth!"

Changing people like changing planes! I hadn't thought of that before, but since that plane ride I have made it a point to take note of the number among us who *are* called upon constantly to "change people" in this separated world. It is astounding!

Society itself thrusts change upon us so rapidly that the innate part of all of us that cries out for stability, roots, and routine barely has time to surface and be comfortably adjusted. Some of it we bring upon ourselves. My parents lived in one house for 36 years; much of today's moving population yawns with the boredom of 36 *months* in one place.

Some causes of stress are a little more subtle. Some psychologists are concluding that one general cause of stress is the lack of motivation, especially among the young. Some go so far as to suggest that a large segment of our country's students merely learn what is taught them without believing or appropriating that knowledge to their lives. While we do hear much pleading for the individual to *be* an individual, conformity is demanded by peers at all ages, and hordes of people wander aimlessly behind the unseen leader.

Without an established code or anticipated goal, stress flourishes and has the upper hand. And it is important to understand that the manifestation of that stress is not always a shaky head or hand. *Depression and inertia are very real side effects of great stress.*

In the Christian body we have added some other dimensions. We struggle over such things as what it is God requires of us, exactly how we can know His will, what the other members of His family think of us, a cautious calculation of the price of an obedient walk with Him, how strong we should be at work, how close we can live to the secular world, just whose interpretation of a controversial scripture is correct, what the no-no's are for us, and on and on.

It is not a pleasant thing to bring up, but alas, the facts insist: Stress is a sure thing when we are not entirely honest before God! I know it is impossible to be less than honest with God without Him knowing it. So why do we try to be? I suppose because we desperately want to believe Satan's lie that God does not mean what He says and in a moment of mercy will turn His head. (See the example of Eve in the Book of Genesis.)

Nothing causes stress in the Christian quicker than the folly of trying to be spiritually what we simply are not. Honesty before God necessitates being in tune with our motive life. And dealing with motive not only forces us to deal with case-building, self-preservation, and "righteous indignation" but also teaches us how to handle these aspects with the kid gloves they require. How old-fashioned to remember that the surest place to accomplish the "correction burns" (to use a space term for redirecting a rocket) motive needs is on our knees. (God seems to have direct access to the heart from the kneebones!)

Since I spend a lot of the time on airplanes with my eyes shut, Don was very surprised (and proud) to see me actually looking intently out the window, soaking in the awesome beauty of upstate New York dressed in its fall wardrobe. It was irresistible. After all, the colors of fall are my favorites, and I was pleased to see the trees were wearing them too. Actually, I was really praying about the speeches that were prepared for the upcoming retreat Don and I were sharing.

"Lord, I want to know that I have ministered to *someone* during these three days. This is too far to fly and too time-consuming not to have made any difference. Lord, this is being done for Your glory. I am not interested in any praise for me."

Suddenly I got very generous with the Lord: "And if only *one* person comes to me afterward to say something complimentary, it's OK."

He shocked me. "Pat, if *no one* says anything, is it *still* for Me?"

Face-to-face with motive. Was the objective really to add spiritual meaning to one life or to perform so that

23

acceptance of me would be ego-pleasing? In that moment only two knew the truth: the Lord and I.

Do you know the word *integrity?* Certainly. It rings a bell of uprightness and sincerity. The dictionary lists it as synonymous with honesty, but then it adds, "undivided or unbroken condition; wholeness, completeness." Smacks of holiness, doesn't it?

Actually, even though integrity is as scarce as a car clock that works, the world looks for it everywhere. Not in the dictionary but in lives.

The Christian life is scrutinized more closely when the world is looking for and expecting integrity than at any other time. And God's children are judged more critically by a watching world in matters requiring integrity than anyone cares to admit. The Christian testimony has no greater opportunity to shine as gold than the one offered at the level of integrity.

Integrity is a noun defined in spirit rather than in word. It is the necessary atom for the building of genuine Christian witness. Somehow conscience bears that out, and *internal* havoc is wrought in the person who ignores or abuses it. When integrity teeters on the edge of compromise, *stress is automatic even before we choose one side of the fence or the other.*

I wrote the preceding sentence with practical experiences of my own in mind. I intended to get one out, dust it off, and share it. But no need. I have a brand-new, fresh one.

Recently I found myself right smack in the middle of one of the toughest teeter-totter episodes of my life. It happened at the beginning of what was to be the fulfillment of a lifelong dream. I was going to visit the United Kingdom, the land of my ancestors. London, Dublin, Edinburgh—all included in a package that would allow me to finally behold the beautiful countrysides painted in my mind of England, Wales, Scotland, and Ireland. With friends Don and Elaine Williams (travel agents) I had helped put together a trip for a small group from our church. We had laid careful and detailed plans.

Thinking it would be nice to start at the church, I arranged for us to go to the airport in a church bus—a little extra fun. Everyone else was on the bus when I arrived. As I boarded, Don, our leader, asked for my passport. I froze. Incredulity blanketed my face—and everyone else's. How could this happen? Every piece of clothing and toiletry had been meticulously collected and packed; traveler's checks and itemized budget were tucked safely in my purse; all home bases that might need my attention while I was gone were covered; but I had not *once* thought of my passport!

No problem; of *course* I had a valid passport!

I jumped off the bus, instructing the group to go on ahead. Since I knew exactly where the passport was, I would go back to the house, pick it up, and meet the excited group at the airport.

Several minutes of searching and rummaging produced nothing but panic. I called my husband. He searched his office. Not there. I searched the drawers and boxes some more. I called him again: "Call the airport. Page Elaine. Tell her it must be in the lid of my suitcase. Tell her to look while I drive to the airport."

I relaxed. My organized mind had planted my suitcase on a spare bed several weeks before and now, mentally, I saw myself dropping in my passport. By the time I walked into the airport I was laughing again. Alas; the faces of those who had just gone through my belongings told me the suitcase search was also futile. Well, I just couldn't go!

Panic again. I could live with the relinquishing of my dream, but I didn't know how to respond to a few who were already declaring they wouldn't be going if I couldn't go.

The airline agent approched. "You will have to tell them in London that you lost your passport en route."

"I can't do that."

She didn't like my answer. "Well, we are not supposed to let you board without it. And unless you or Mr. Williams tell them at customs that you lost it on your way they will send you back to the United States on the first plane at *your* expense!"

No sympathy!

She and Mr. Williams conferred. I was given permission to go. One thing now was for sure: I would at least get to London.

I looked at my watch: 45 minutes until takeoff. I called my husband's office again. "Go to the house. I may have missed some place. Call me at this pay phone." He did. I hadn't!

Our concerned group flew to Minneapolis. I was sorry for the damper my forgetfulness had cast on our joy. The heaviness followed me to my seat on the Jumbo Jet. Which was the greater burden: the distress I had caused everyone, or the prospect of continuing by way of a lie? I honestly could not remember ever lying about anything. Probably as a child I must have, but even before becoming a Christian it was against my religion.

Not far into the night I realized Satan had the same seat assignment. He began his onslaught on my integrity, and I began a night of stress and anguish.

"I can't lie to them!"

He answered with important considerations: "A lot of these people are on this tour because of *you.* You *can't* let them down. After all, you *do* have a valid passport; it isn't as if you are trying to put something over on someone or *intentionally* doing something illegal. God *certainly* understands. Anyway, how come He didn't bring it to your memory?"

"I can't *lie* to them!"

"You are being foolish. Everyone will understand your predicament and will recognize it's the only thing you can do."

The long hours of the night stretched out before me, as did the hundreds of miles between the safe shores of my homeland and the unknown face waiting at a customs desk. I was a bundle of stress.

Toward morning I opened my Bible, asking the Lord to let my eyes fall on a verse pertinent to my situation. He did. *Pertinent* it was!

> He that saith, I know him, and keepeth not his commandments, is a liar, and the truth is not in him. But whoso keepeth his word, in him verily is the love of God perfected: hereby know we that we are in him *(1 John 2:4-5).*

It was not what I wanted or expected, but it certainly got the job done!

"OK, Lord, You don't have to draw me a picture."

I climbed over sleeping bodies and found my way to a seat next to Don and Elaine. Don is a man of high integrity, and I noticed he had not slept either.

"Don," I began, "I haven't slept all night. I've been praying, and God has given me a verse."

He smiled with a hint of relief. "I have had a great struggle, too. And He has given *me* a verse!" He read:

> I waited patiently for the Lord; and he inclined unto me, and heard my cry *(Ps. 40:1)*.

"Tell you what we are going to do," I answered. "God has shown me that I have no choice but to tell the truth. I cannot lie, nor can I let you. Besides, this struggle tonight has shown me that the whole two weeks would be ruined knowing I had entered the country illegally."

As I talked, a strength poured through my being. I knew it was God. The power that comes from making a decision of integrity is God's vote of approval coupled with the triumph of one's own self-respect.

"The rest of you go on through customs. I have prayed that God will direct me to the right official. I'll simply tell him the truth, and God will take care of the outcome, one way or another."

Never shall I forget the sensation I felt while walking down the ramp that led into the huge customs area adjacent to the London airport. I hadn't dreamed there would be so many checkpoints.

One more time I pleaded: "Lord, show me where to go!"

My eyes scanned the long row of officials and came to rest on a gentleman almost in the middle. The Lord gave a nudge, and I got in line. All too quickly it was my turn.

"I don't have a passport," I declared to the very startled face.

"OH, DEAR!" (A decided English accent.) "Where is it?"

"I don't know," I admitted.

"Did you have it at the airport in the United States?" (Right to the nitty-gritty!)

"No, sir."

"You mean they let you out of the country *without* it?" His eyes said, *"Shame* on them."

28

"Yes, sir."

"You don't know where it is?"

"No, sir. I could not find it at the last minute after searching for it at home to no avail. I decided it must be in my suitcase already at the airport, but it wasn't. The agent in Denver told me to tell you I lost it on my way, but I can't do that because it is not the truth."

(There, Lord, I said it!)

Again with amazement: "They let you out of the country *without* it?"

Only the lump and dryness in my throat kept me from laughing.

He asked for identification. Could I prove I was who I said I was? He asked my friend Don, who had cleared customs and now stood nearby, if he would swear as to my identity. Did he see me on a regular basis? I smiled a little at Don's psychology: "Yes, sir, every Sunday in church!"

The official reached for a form. He smiled.

"How tall are you?"

"Five feet 6 inches. You aren't going to ask my weight, are you?"

Well . . . never mind, this story is getting too long.

After lots of writing, a loud thump imprinted an official stamp on a piece of paper, and the gentleman handed me a document allowing me to travel freely for 60 days!

"Have a good time," were his parting words. If he only knew!

We walked from his desk out of the room and around a corner to join our waiting companions. They were all crying. Someone said reverently, "Praise the Lord," and we worshiped together. It was appropriate: It was Sunday morning.

Honesty before God includes a recognition of our

needs and a dependence upon Him to meet those needs. The healthier my relationship, the less stressful it will be, and vice versa. *My relationship with God is as healthy as the degree of my dependence on Him.* John 15:5 reads, "He that abideth in me, and I in him, the same bringeth forth much fruit: for *without me* ye can do nothing" (italics added throughout). If I can do things in my own strength, I am not abiding. And the moment I cease to abide in Him my spirit becomes restless, then frustrated and anxious. If not promptly attended to, these upheavals will cause me to shy away from God.

A man once asked J. G. Morrison, "How little religion can a man have and still get to heaven?"

His provoking answer: "Just enough to be comfortable in the presence of Jesus!"

Another consideration: Stress is *consistently* a by-product of our failure to adjust to the inequities and injustices of life. Mark it down: Life never has been, is not now, and never will be fair! I doubt that any negative concept has more positive results when understood and accepted than that one.

A very popular song became exactly that a few years ago because it hit a collective nerve in the population. It reprimanded complaint by simply stating, "I never promised you a rose garden." What did you expect? Surely not that life would live up to hopes and dreams and fairness?

If we give our permission, the "unfairness" of a given situation, or the injustice prevalent all around us will precipitate immeasurable stress. It will eat at us until it gnaws away a large chunk of our rationale. Soon our thinking is colored red, white, and blue: angry, frightened, and depressed.

Unfairness is *not* the punishment doled out to the sinner, as we sometimes wish it were. We do well to remind ourselves of that *often.* I even dared to remind a friend recently. Two of her close family members were living drastically different lives. How agonizing to see the one who was a fine Christian suffering and struggling with a terminal illness, and how unfair to watch the one who had turned his back on God make lots of money and enjoy riotous living and good health! Her consuming stress had side-tracked her faith and blinded her to the fact that God, *because* of His justice, loved them both. How we as on-lookers would love to reverse the rewards.

When unfairness and injustice are flourishing around us, the cry of the heart is "What can be done? What can I DO?" The questions are not a disgrace. But to be consumed and conquered by asking and answering is a one-way, futile conversation, and God is not pleased. The predicament is only compounded because we eliminate most of what we *could* do by anxiety over that about which we can do nothing. Satan is delighted to see us drain ourselves of precious physical energy and to drown spiritual vitality in stress. What a web we weave when we doggedly pursue the "whys."

Well, there's no doubt about it, stress is alive and well and perching on our doorstep. Not all stress is harmful, of course, but most of the time it is. Certainly it is conceded that none of us is, or can be, entirely stress free. Some seem to come close, but the fact is that the majority of us still need to learn how to prevent the inner emotional stress and anxiety we are so susceptible to from becoming a tool in Satan's hand capable of destroying a victorious, every-day walk with Christ.

Let's discuss the inevitable question: What is stress?

Stress itself is not a disease. It is not usually an isolated event. Nor is it a collection of problems. Strictly speaking, stress is a *compilation of responses*, sometimes few, sometimes many, *based more in perception than in activity!* Whether or not it is associated more with activity or inactivity is a circular argument.

By studying the life of Jesus, we know stress cannot simply be busyness. Jesus was very busy. His mission and nature demanded it. True, sometimes very busy people succumb to stress. Yet some of the busiest people in the world are more devoid of stress than most. Experts explain that, in part, in terms of good organization, priority systems that work, and good evaluations of the important and the trivial. A little disgusting, isn't it? I wish I could take a huge dose of organization along with the vitamin B_{12}!

My parents were frequent and welcome visitors to our home. Father, after astute observation, once remarked, "You know, your generation has more buttons to push, more gadgets to work for you, more conveniences at your fingertips than any other generation; yet you are the busiest women in history." As he left for home he added, "Honey, please don't do the washing at midnight anymore!"

But then, people of little activity or adequacy are not guaranteed immunity from breakdowns. People who have never done anything have them. For one thing, *inactivity is often the breeding ground of self-deprecation and its resultant anxiety.* It isn't fiction that an idle mind is the devil's workshop. It is in reality a mental jungle.

The *World Book Dictionary* defines stress as pressure, force, and strain. We understand those words pretty well. Let me suggest another concept.

Science tells us the universe operates on the principle of cause and effect. There is action and result, motive and consequence, initiative and response. I believe that stress is the *preoccupation with the effect without properly or sufficiently dealing with the cause.*

Jesus constantly dealt with cause. Recall the incident of the woman taken in adultery. Those around were intolerant of her degradation and angry with her and what she represented. Jesus reached beyond their emotions, even past the effect on her life, and addressed himself directly to the cause.

"Go, and sin no more," He spoke in forgiveness (John 8:11).

The disciples thought Him uncaring when He bypassed their fear of drowning and spoke simply to the raging Sea of Galilee. "Peace, be still," He instructed, and the "cause" obeyed (Mark 4:39).

Jesus met the challenge of life at the very heart of it. To be fruitful and successful we, too, must learn to deal with causes. Trouble is, dealing with causes calls for discipline. Why is it that in all of life that crazy word keeps popping up?

During a recent lunch conversation a friend commented that the number one health problem in America was obesity. (Glad I ordered the fruit plate!)

"No," I philosophized, "the number one problem with Americans is our atrocious lack of discipline." (One finger pointed at me.)

It really is easier sometimes to endure the frustration of stress or to bounce around in the throes of indecision than to *exercise the discipline needed to rout out the cause*. Or at least for the time being it seems easier.

Even the causes of stress classified as trivial need our

attention. Personality and behavior so easily settle into certain patterns that become harder to change as time goes by. Sometimes we refer to people as "set in their ways," usually about little things. Little things become engrained because we see them as not worthy of discipline.

Whatever the cause for stress, it will not just go away. Oh, it may retreat for the moment or for the present, but we can be very sure it will come back at a later day and will continue to reappear until we identify it and deal with it.

Now we are at the beginning of very basic psychology. The first step of discipline in dealing with stress is to identify its cause. That needs to be done whether we are suffering a small misunderstanding or an overwhelming set of messy problems. Name it. Tag it. *Drifting,* all by itself, *produces great stress.* Some people waste more energy in stress over what they need to be doing than it eventually takes to do the job itself!

But it is no mystery why we humans shy away from dealing with and identifying causes. A great deal of the time the search leads us right to our own doorstep—our own doing. A lot of stress is brought about because we ignore the existent knowledge we have of ourselves.

Too often we stray outside the individual personality fences that protect our stability because we do not like what we see *in our own backyard.* The greener grass beyond is not only deceptive but also just a stopgap! A gentleman who knows told me recently that the grass is only greener until you eat it.

Discipline shores up the yard and fence at home first of all. The Texans where we used to pastor had a wonderful, parochial expression: "Tend to your own rat killin'." That summed it up pretty well on many occasions.

"Cause" is sometimes a very evident thing. But for all

sorts of reasons, many of us have the propensity to circle the core like circling the maypole.

It is amazing what women tell their hairdressers. Isn't it a wonder that having one's hair washed also loosens the tongue. I suppose that kind of free exchange establishes a certain kind of "unattached" friendship.

I don't share intimate things with mine, but I have to admit to a degree of freedom that is unusual for me. In fact, I was downright shocked at myself recently when I sat down in her chair and unhesitantly said, "Don't ask me how I want my hair today. Just do it. And don't ask me how I am. I'm not up to conversation!"

She was a little surprised, too. As she laughed, I looked in the mirror and sighed. Just as I suspected, I looked 100 years old, which is 3 or 4 more than I admit to.

She began to brush and I began to talk—inwardly.

"I'm absolutely, totally, and completely frustrated and fed up, and cannot go on. In fact, I am *two weeks* past the point of going on. I know what I will do. I will stand up, collapse, and let them carry me off to the hospital, and I'll sleep for days. They can feed me intravenously, and I'll wake up when I get good and ready!"

Both my hands and legs were shaking as I walked to the shampoo chair and closed my eyes. How I wished I could count sheep! Instead I counted all the remaining things I had to do that day. Gradually, I began to reflect on the things I had not done. There had been no listening to God's "slow down" warnings or acknowledging of His tap on the shoulder. I hadn't prayed. I hadn't read His Word, being just "too busy." I hadn't allowed time for the slightest restoration of my physical or spiritual strength.

Long ago God had shown me the boundaries of my stamina. It had been a clear, painful, but sure lesson. When will I ever admit that there is a limit to which my physical energy can be stretched? Why have I made the extension of that limit the standard rather than the exception? And why pretend ignorance when the body and mind are so exhausted that stress is exceedingly abundant and in control? Would He again touch and help me with my humanness? I prayed that He would.

The cause! Staring me right in the face. The cure? God did touch me that afternoon, calming the stressful spirit and giving an added portion of strength. Yet I wonder if it was coincidence that a few days later I contracted a minor illness and in recuperation slept and slept and slept?

Discipline demands action. Sometimes that is as simple as using one's brain. Occasionally it requires a remolding of the vessel. Once in a while it necessitates a complete change of life-style. But it *always* requires the determination of the will.

When I have confronted cause, then I must act!

I've never been too responsive to Bible verses with an optional ring, preferring the definite dos and don'ts. One very meaningful, oft-used scripture I used to consider a "maybe" is John 14:1. I suppose because ministers and their wives attend lots of funerals, I have heard that verse more than many have.

I would never have been disrespectful enough to do this, but in years past while listening to a minister intone, "Let not your heart be troubled . . . ," I've been tempted to stand and ask, "All well and good. Just how do I do that? I don't *want* my heart to be troubled."

Then one day, while engaged in an in-depth study of the Gospel of John, I read that the original manuscripts of that verse indicate it should read, "*Choose* to cease being troubled." *Choose* to deal with it. I liked that! For, even though that put some responsibility on me, it was thrilling to know that I could, and should, take some definite steps to deal with my troubled, anxious self.

And I could offer that as a kickoff for recovery to my bereaved friends. Sorrow and separation perpetuate stress, such causes being easily identified in death. Yet we have the privilege to deal with its stress by the action choice provides. Discipline is so often neglected in sorrow.

Choice is such a God-given premium. Probably none of us comprehends fully its expanse or significance. And the magnitude of choice as the result of *His* direction, coupled with *His* promised help, is absolutely breathtaking! Choice, His direction, and His help positions me at an unequaled vista. Nowhere do I see opportunity more clearly. I have the prerogative to cash in the coupons.

Lewis T. Corlett, in a wonderful book titled *Holiness in Practical Living,* spoke about the impact of choice.

> Now life with all of its activities and backgrounds is seen as the handiwork of God, whereas formerly (before regeneration) little thought was given to God's place in the universe. Out of these changes in the life comes a strong desire, on the part of the child of God, to grow in grace and to become more like his Master every day.
>
> While these are all good, yet the Christian must continually make choices in daily life to keep his life in harmony both with all that God has done in him and also in agreement with the first decisions of the will that were made by the individual to prepare for God's operations in his heart. Good character is built by a process of right choices. Holiness in the heart and life of the believer is maintained and increased by a process of choices in harmony with God's will and purpose.

Though a layman in psychology, may I suggest some basic steps of such?

We choose to *identify* cause by discipline's help, and

we choose to *isolate* that cause by deliberate action. What does it mean to "isolate"? Very simply, it means to separate the cause of negative stress from daily thought and activity. It does not mean to ignore or to give up in despair when we feel powerless to change. But we do choose to hold at arm's length the cause we have identified. The circumstances shall not consume our minds and short-circuit our productivity.

We identify, we isolate, and, when possible, we replace. Didn't you know I would get to the point of divine involvement? God's Word is chuck full of positives for replacing negatives. He always has an alternative, a cure, a promise, a healing balm, a blessing, or strength—or all of the above when needed!

We don't want to imply that life is a simple ABC recital, but it certainly is easier when we care enough to face it and do something about it. God wants only to know that we consider our lives worthy of *work*.

Now we come to *faith*. Dealing with causes must incorporate some degree of faith. Jesus had ultimate faith. What insight we embrace when we admit that sooner or later anxiety and stress must be replaced by faith! Not to come to that conclusion seriously hampers our relationship to Christ.

> The message they heard was of no value to them, because those who heard did not combine it with faith *(Heb. 4:2, NIV)*.

The writer of Hebrews, though speaking about the message of the gospel, inadvertently gave us a rule of thumb for judging the status of any spiritual tenet. Has it reached the crossroads of faith, and which path has it taken?

Praise the Lord that the discipline of action brings us to the bridge of faith. *Every spiritual truth gets to this point at some time or other.* Crossing that bridge should be as natural for the Christian as breathing. We need not even calculate what lies on the other side. We never have reason to fear the territory of faith. Our steps on the ground of faith should be the firmest walk we ever experience. The Bible says, "Having done all, . . . stand" (Eph. 6:13). We have not done all until we have embraced faith.

Faith makes it possible to "Let the peace of Christ rule in your hearts" (Col. 3:15, NIV).

"Be [anxious] for nothing," Paul says, "but in every thing by prayer and supplication with thanksgiving let your requests be made known unto God" (Phil. 4:6).

Overpowering the "nothing" of anxiety should be the "everything" of prayer! Could it be that simple?

Not long ago I read one man's opinion of what that verse in Philippians means. He dared to propose that to allow ourselves to be harassed by care is in reality a kind of practical atheism! He may have a point, in that when the world does not see us handling anxiety and stress very well, it concludes we are no better off than nonbelievers.

Anxiety, indeed, has a very distorted memory. It will not let us forget that similar situations have turned out badly; it delights in reminding us that we are not in control; and it convinces us that all our fears and apprehensions will surely come to pass.

That's why God's antidote is a good dose of *intimate prayer and thanksgiving.* Today's anxiety is dealt a great blow by remembering what He has done for us yesterday. Thanksgiving chases anxiety out the back door to swelter in the hot sun of faithlessness!

Robert Louis Stevenson once said, "He who is no longer thankful has fallen asleep in life." Could I possibly go to sleep in the midst of anxiety?

Ah, we come full circle to peace. Verse 7 of Philippians, chapter 4, is an assurance that, after prayer and thanksgiving, "the peace of God, which passeth all understanding, shall keep your hearts and minds through Christ Jesus." The apostle Paul was not a soldier, yet he used a military term to picture God's stance as He keeps our hearts and minds.

The Greek word here for "keep" means one who is standing guard with a trained, watchful eye. The enemy cannot have access. God's peace is a sentinel, strong enough to turn back Satan's armies of frustration, worry, anxiety, nervousness, and stress.

God deals in strength. This is no tin soldier guarding our hearts and minds. If we care enough to appropriate God's formula of discipline, action, trust, and thanksgiving, we are guarded by a full-blown, steel-cast battalion! His peace will put metal in our substance.

How exemplary Jesus was for us. His was a life of unquestioned integrity and honesty before His Father. He disciplined himself to the identification of cause. He acted on truth. He walked from the manger to the Cross through repeated onslaughts of external stress and available anxiety and steadfastly refused to be conquered by either. He marched on the solid ground of faith, a march that provided Him with the authority to offer us a special kind of peace: one that is honey to the soul, music to the ears, and a life-rope for modern man!

2

His Peace Was Separate from External Circumstances and Relationships

Peace I leave with you; my peace I give you. I do not give to you as the world gives. Do not let your hearts be troubled and do not be afraid (*John 14:27, NIV*).

It seems to me that Jesus could have chosen a more likely time and atmosphere in which to offer us His peace. There are so many pastoral places in Israel that could have better served as a backdrop for those precious words. But no, for some reason He chose the Upper Room in Jerusalem. If the Upper Room in which He spoke resembled the one I saw in the Holy City, its starkness was not conducive to either inspiration or peace.

And what of Jerusalem itself? Hostility robed the city. The forces of evil were gathering as swiftly and ominously as the eye of a hurricane. Preparations for this confrontation with the Son of God had been going on for centuries. Jesus knew that. Wisely, He had at times avoided Jerusalem because, as He had told His mother, "Mine hour is not yet come" (John 2:4; see 7:30; 8:20). But now the hour *had* come (12:23, 27; 13:1; 17:1). History waited with wooden arms. Jesus was not duped by the recent shouts of adulation from the crowds or lulled into fantasy by the breeze of the palm branches. He knew that He was in the Holy City for one reason: to die!

Nothing fills me with such dreadful emotion as watching a convicted criminal being led step by step to execution. Reading the details in the morning paper gives me goosebumps, and watching by way of television is sickening. What must that one be feeling? Could there possibly be a crime that offers enough thrill or revenge to be worth dying for? I've tried to conjecture just how I would feel knowing that my feet, one after the other, were taking me to my last breath? I shudder. I have imagined that I would scream, kick, fight, and in desperation find enough supernatural strength to release myself from my captors! And RUN!

Condemned! That is exactly the mood and circumstance in which Jesus gently and generously said, "Peace I leave with you; my peace I give you." How utterly incredible. This Man was one gasp away from what the world thought was His destruction. Little did they know. But Jesus knew. He felt, yet He still offered. And His offer is valid today because *His gift was not determined, sustained, or altered by the external.* His sacrificial death blazed the message across the skies of the centuries that those of us who believe on Him can enjoy a peace that need not be uprooted by stormy, evil forces, or by the nitty-gritty per-plexities of everyday living.

This is a great place to quote Dr. Earl Lee. In a recent conversation with him, my heart was moved to hear him declare, "We do not have to be subject to outward circum-stance." Knowing that he came to that conclusion while his son was an Iranian hostage gave his words depth and au-thority, and I whispered to myself, "Praise the Lord!"

In case we are tempted to minimize the external world that Jesus withstood, we need only to recall such adjec-tives as *unbelieving, skeptical, scoffing, blasphemous, hateful, mocking, hypocritical,* and *determined.* Furthermore, most of those who followed Him were not sincere seekers, just curiosity hounds waiting anxiously to exploit His powers.

The Crucifixion left the disciples a motley bunch—not that any of us would not have been. They were con-fused and at loose ends. The nails of the Roman soldiers had turned their world upside down. That world could now resound with "I told you so!" And so it was that Jesus, after the Resurrection, patiently reiterated to them what His kingdom was all about. He stood in their midst and triumphantly declared, "Peace be with you!" My kingdom is not one of the sword or of political maneuvering, nor does it belong to the skeptic. Never mind the unbelief of a scoffing world; never mind the scheming of the Jews and Pharisees; never mind that, so far, you have been a pitiful minority; never mind that you will not rule an earthly, po-litical kingdom. Those are merely external pestilences un-able to nullify the inner well of divine peace flowing freely from the divine experience. "I have overcome the world" (John 16:33).

And the message hasn't changed one iota. God, through Christ, pours into the hearts of His children that same substance called peace. It still remains capable of surviving illness, divorce, unhappy marriage, financial reverses, poverty, prosperity, unwanted singleness, the challenges of single parenthood, injustice, disability, and the whole kit and caboodle.

It is more than a "gritting of the teeth" determination; more than resolutely thinking positively; more than hanging on and hanging on; more than martyrdom; and infinitely more than the humanistic "I can do it myself" philosophy. It is a gift; it is God-given; it is tested; it is a by-product of a personal, intimate relationship between God and an individual; it is guaranteed by Christ's integrity; it is planted deep; and it is *available*.

I have found it to be intact myself over many years of ups and downs, sideways and acrosses.

I have seen it painted on the canvases of many lives. May I present a couple of portraits to you?

June came to a women's retreat. Our paths crossed for a short two days, but the enrichment to my life will last forever. Though knowing nothing about her at the time, I knew beyond doubt that her smile bore the marks of one who had been through the fire. It was a silent shout of victory.

June had been a Christian only about a year. Her 28 years had been lived in a traditional way. She had settled into a comfortable routine of being wife and mother, had willingly taken a job to supplement her husband's income, and anticipated the day they could buy a house. The everyday schedule of working, picking up her son at the sitter's, arriving home to fix supper, and spending the evenings "catching up" was not boring to her.

The day that changed her life was no different until the turn of the key opened her front door, and she stepped across its threshold into a completely empty house. No furniture, no pictures on the walls. Instinctively she raced to the kitchen to call the police. There she found the note. Its words became blurred as she read, and its message screamed at her: John had left . . . someone else . . . forget . . . something about love . . . no chance . . . She walked through the house as if hoping to find a prankster in a closet. But the closets contained only her clothes and those of her child. She went to the cupboards. They, too, had been stripped of their belongings. One box of crackers stood alone.

Here are her words: "Pat, I knew there was nothing I could do about the situation that night. My pride kept me from calling the few I knew who might care. I was thankful for the crackers; my legs would not have taken me to the store. I took my little boy, wrapped him in my coat, and sat down on the living room floor; and as I fed him a box of crackers, I rocked and sang until he fell asleep. *But I was not alone!* There was a Presence that filled the empty room to overflowing and a peace that came to my heart that was indescribable. And believe it or not, I slept!"

The following morning June confirmed with the bank what she had suspected the night before: John had taken not only the household belongings but also the money from their checking and savings accounts as well.

Let her words encourage you: "I called my employer to say I wouldn't be working that day. Actually, I really didn't know *what* I was going to be doing. But as I weighed the possibilities, the doorbell rang. I opened the door to a casual acquaintance who lived about two blocks away. Her arms could barely hold two brown bags. She was not a Christian, so I'm sure she didn't realize what she *really* was saying. 'I have no idea why I am here, but I want you to have these groceries,' she said."

June smiled her smile of victory as she continued. "That was nine months ago, and I have not really needed a thing since then. And that tremendous peace has not left me for one tiny moment!"

What can I say?

Just as I typed that question, some lyrics from a lingering childhood song found their way to my fingers

It's just like Jesus to roll the clouds away.
It's just like Jesus to keep me day by day.

I must tell you about Ruie. That name is probably a new one to you. It's unusual, like the lady who bears it. She is one of those unobtrusive, behind-the-scenes witnesses who make up so much of the core of God's army.

Everyone who knows her knows about her faith. That included her doctors. In the weeks preceding her open-heart surgery she found ample opportunity to tell them about her God. Consequently, her Jewish doctor was not just being funny when he told his colleagues, "Now, you must do a great job on Ruie. Her God will be watching, and I don't want Him saying, 'Look at those monkeys down there!'"

But I'm ahead of the story.

Ruie and I first said hello in a Sunday School class I was teaching. Nothing about her betrayed the fact that only a short 10 days before, she had tried to end her life. She was lovely and charming, and one would have to look closely to detect that she was hesitant and unsure. Going to an evangelical church was strange to her, and the people she found there were certainly different from other acquaintances.

She was there (I found out later) because of a caring

brother. The hospital, having saved her life, had sent her back to the same empty house and "dead-end streets" from which she had come. She decided she would just not get out of bed. And that's exactly where her brother found her that Sunday morning. He knew what she needed. He *literally* took her out of bed, dressed her, and brought her to church.

Like a carefully tended rosebud, Ruie responded to the message of God's grace and the love of His family. Soon she invited the Savior into her heart and began to blossom into the lovable person she is today.

I concluded early that Ruie was not basically suicidal. As she became involved in the ministry of the church, I was astounded to see the range of talent that was hers. I could not imagine that life could have driven her to such drastic action. But after learning the facts, I wondered if I, too, would not have been tempted to end it all.

The facts. Here they are in their ugliness.

For a husband of 30 years to forsake his wife for a woman half his age is not a new story. (Sad, but true.) In Ruie's case, however, the woman was her best friend, and the secret rendezvous had been aided and abetted by her own daughter. For over two years father, daughter, and best friend had been cohorts.

Barely staggering to her feet from that blow, Ruie discovered that she not only was facing a divorce but was going to be subjected to a nasty financial battle as well. Her husband intended to claim all their considerable assets. Blow number two.

Number three was the discovery that none of the lawyers she knew would represent her. Her husband was too well known for them to risk a professional friendship, and

47

she found it difficult to find a qualified attorney who did not recognize her name. She gave in to futility.

Remember the Sunday School class? Ruie came that first Sunday, unfamiliar with anything we talked about. During the discussion of the morning I mentioned the word *consecration*. Casually, because it was not related at the time, I added, "We don't have time to explore that today, but—"

One of the men spoke up. "Pat," he interjected, "I wish we would *take* time. I know of nothing I need to understand more than consecration and what it means."

I hesitated. I didn't want to be diverted from the lesson at hand. But I agreed we would look into it. I kept that promise, and the next Sunday we began what turned out to be a 10-month discussion! We scrutinized and dissected every word that was related: *consecration, dedication, set apart, commitment, sanctification, Spirit-filled, Christian perfection*. On and on. At one point I confided to the Lord: "Lord, please help our group to bring this to a close. I want to get on with other stuff."

Finally we put a collective period on our study. Done! And God taught me an unforgettable lesson. That morning Ruie waited past the dismissal prayer. Her eyes were free of concern, and her face looked as if she had found a magical fountain of youth!

"You know," she began, "I go to court tomorrow supposedly for the last time. I have asked the Lord repeatedly why this ordeal has taken 10 months. Now I know why. Just this morning I have come to the point of commitment where I can say that it doesn't matter what happens tomorrow. Today I have relinquished it all to Him. It is absolutely and forever in His hands. I have *great* peace!"

The next day I waited for her call. I needn't have answered the phone, for I knew in my heart what she would say.

"Would you believe that the court gave me everything I asked for?" She laughed a beautiful laugh. "My attorney wondered why I was so different. I told him I had just brought the Lord along!"

I would love to tell you that life has been a bed of roses for Ruie since then, that she has been living happily ever after, that God has given her someone new to love, and that she has no cares. But I can't. Hers is no fairy tale. Since her divorce she has had complete kidney failure necessitating continual dialysis, she has had the heart surgery I referred to earlier, she has had difficult financial problems, and a massive stroke has left her with slow speech and faltering feet. A walker is her new companion.

Yet she has so much. With her permission to share this story comes a P.S. from her: There is a peace from God more precious than health, and it is separate from external circumstances. It exists on a much higher plane than heartache or physical discomfort.

Perhaps the most dreaded external circumstance is death. How beautiful to know that for the Christian, death is just exactly that: external. Certainly it hurts inwardly, but it is still *strictly external.* That is a big part of the mystery about it that we do not comprehend. But even death cannot squeeze from us that inner peace given by Christ.

One Saturday morning I was enjoying a backyard, storybook brunch. I would be hard pressed to arrange a more beautiful morning. The sun was bright, and the clouds melted like ice cream across the sky and parted at just the right intervals to reveal the pink-hued mountains. They in turn lifted tiny globs of snowy whipped cream to the blue sky. As if that wasn't enough to satisfy an aesthetic soul, the food, looking like a *Good Housekeeping* centerfold, lazily spread itself over a large table, beckoning the guests to enjoy. I was with very delightful people, and civilization was millions of miles away—well, not quite. Ma Bell knows where everybody is!

The hostess called me to the phone. As I listened the sun and I found a dark cloud. My brother, from a western state, broke the news that Mother had suffered a massive stroke the night before and had not regained consciousness. Of course, I would get there as soon as I could.

"As soon as I could" turned out to be very late at night. It was after midnight when I walked into a small hospital room to join my family in a loving vigil that Mother probably knew nothing about.

I decided to spend the nights at her bedside. Many times, as a child, I had heard Mother say she hated being alone at night.

Mother had a private room simply because one bed was its capacity. It was a tiny room, indeed. Trying to be comfortable, I situated two chairs so that by curling my legs around the arm of one I was "sort of" lying down. Not a good way to sleep. In fact, sleep was impossible.

The second night the strain and activity of the previous two days finally took their toll. I was very weary and decided that the curves of my body and those of the chairs just weren't compatible. I gave up and sat up. Then I began to take stock of my surroundings. The external!

Everything in the room seemed to be gray, including Mother. As I walked to her side, I thought, When did she get so old? She had always been so young. Oh, somewhere in my mental file I knew her birth certificate had been written 78 years before, but that had held no relevance for me until now. With surprise I noticed how aged her skin had become.

I began a nostalgic rundown of some of the places she and I had been together. We had picked out lots of pretty dresses; for the first time I realized 98 percent of them had been for me. We had combined our talents on lots of cakes and pies and cookies; she made them, I ate them. Together we had planned a lovely wedding: mine. She had helped me raise a couple of children and in the process taught me that being a grandmother meant "being there" when a young mother is all thumbs. We had stood side by side weeping over the casket of a man we both loved dearly: my father.

Suddenly, in the midst of reminiscing came the awareness again of that peace that is beyond explaining. Amazing, amazing! In this tiny room, dreary in its decor and limitations, I was spending a farewell service with one of the dearest persons in my life, and *there was peace!*

A few nights later she and I shared again. Not an experience, for I could not go with her when she exchanged earthly oxygen for a sweeter atmosphere; but we shared an indescribable peace, each in her own way. And out of that precious peace came the joyful realization that we would share the resurrection, too!

I know Jesus, in His humanity, sweat great drops of blood in Gethsemane. But that agony did not alter the gift of peace. In truth, Gethsemane assures it. How else could Paul write without challenge, "O death, where is thy sting? O grave, where is thy victory?" (1 Cor. 15:55).

Charles Swindoll has written wisely: "We are all faced with a series of great opportunities brilliantly disguised as unsolvable problems."

The external is, of course, a reflection of the internal.

But the deep internal resource of the heart determines what influence the external shall have. The "unsolvable problems" are inescapable. The Master taught us they can remain *external*.

I have written in my Bible an in-a-nutshell truth from Dr. Edward Lawlor: "Life is *lived* looking forward. It is *understood* looking backward." The beauty is that, whether looking forward or backward, we see God's gift of peace existing apart from and in spite of external circumstances.

That brings us back to where we started: in the Upper Room. May we forget for the moment that Jesus was facing death? Dining with loved ones is a special enjoyment. Even burned beans or dry toast is palatable when shared with friends. Jesus was not the exception. I'm sure His psyche found nourishment in fellowship. Yet at that feast in the Upper Room Judas was not the only traitor on the guest list. Eventually the list would number 12.

You may disagree, but I believe the agony of knowing that His most intimate followers would soon forsake Him must have been on a par with the dread of the Cross itself. One by one, these disciples would disperse back into the world from which our Lord had called them even before the wood that was to outline His body was securely in place. This would be no small heartache! Being forsaken by a friend or loved one is one of life's most disappointing affairs. Multiply that by 12. Add the invested time and subtract His hope for them. The sum total is rejection that hurts and hurts.

Jesus knew that just around the corner the Cross would be His lone companion. I wonder if He felt like banging the table and reminding those 12 of the lost condition He had rescued them from? Did He feel the need to grab them by the lapels and demand the loyalty He so deserved? (After all, He would shortly give His life for them.)

I think not. These excerpts from His conversation cause us to scratch our heads in wonderment:

> I do not give to you as the world gives. . . . remain in my love . . . Love each other as I have loved you. Greater love has no one than this, that he lay down his life for his friends. You are my friends . . . the Counselor, the Holy Spirit, whom the Father will send in my name, will teach you all things and will remind you of everything I have said to you. . . . my peace I give *(John 14:27; 15:10, 12-14; 14:26-27, NIV)*.

Ever have a trusted friend betray you, or a dependable Christian forsake the faith? I'm not talking about superficial relationships; I'm talking about those whose lives have been so intertwined with yours that even your punctuation marks are compatible! If your answer is no, get on your knees and spend a great deal of time thanking the Lord. Then get up and get fortified! Sometime it will happen.

I'm glad it happened to me when I was young. At the time I didn't think of myself as being young and vulnerable, but today I realize how young and unprepared I really was. Even though it still happens and I must still go to my knees, I'm thankful the *argument* about it was settled back then.

I'm ashamed to admit now that that first great betrayal almost cost my spiritual life. I came close to losing my way permanently. Why? Why? Why? I asked. The void sent back, Who cares? Who cares? Who cares? It ceased to be a question and became a statement; and I was in trouble!

Weeks of depression robbed me of so many things. Thank God for everlasting, divine patience. I didn't deserve deliverance, but one day as my hand and hurt pushed a broom across the kitchen floor with a vengeance, the Master Healer quoted His Word: "What is that to thee? follow thou me" (John 21:22).

It was not a command; it was an invitation. It was presented as a shield, a "bullet-proof" vest if you please, an impregnable fortress against the armies of faithless, fickle humanity. My cry of "What's the use?" disappeared. In its place came a renewed resolution to serve the Lord no matter what others did. In no way would another's faithlessness be allowed to derail me. That poor broom handle. I nearly squeezed it to death!

I don't want to tell you how many years ago that has been. You wouldn't believe someone my age could remember so well! Anyway, I prefer the updated. Just yesterday I prayed compassionately for someone who has disappointed and hurt me greatly. It's pure conjecture, of course, but I'm just sure I saw a smile break out on the Lord's face. With a nod of the head He murmured, "Pat, you just might make it yet!"

Can we absorb into the inner fiber of the mind, emotion, and will that there is no circumstance of life, no external trial, no excruciating experience beyond the reach of God's help? Not mere interest, but *help*. If we can lean hard on His everlasting arms, His understanding, and His empathy, we can survive without any other prop.

Dr. William Barclay knew about all of this long before I discovered it. He wrote:

> The peace which Jesus offers us is the peace of conquest. It is the peace which no experience in life can ever take from us. It is the peace which no sorrow, no danger, no suffering can make less. It is the peace which is independent of outward circumstance.

Indeed! No small thing is this gift of peace. It dares proclaim itself equal to everything and anything external. But can it live up to expectation? Oh, yes! Try it. You will join the millions who have tested it against every imaginable external circumstance. They will welcome the addition of your voice as they sing peacefully, "It is well with my soul!"

3

His Peace Was a Result of Obedience to the Father's Will

Now, I am not a theologian, and I dare not speak for them. But as for me and my house, we do not have a complete (key word) grasp of the essence of the Trinity. Oh, I can explain the rudiments of the Three in One and give a substantial biblical bibliography, but I must confess that I cannot comprehend it in its entirety! You see, my mind is so earthly. All substances I know about are singular in their overall function. Everyone in my world operates as an individual. Oh, to be sure, each individual has many component parts, but not one of those parts is capable of leaving the whole and operating on its own. Yet the Bible teaches us that the Father, Son, and Holy Spirit can do that and still be One.

Witness the holy occasion of the baptism of Jesus, the Son. The Spirit descended as a dove, and the Father spoke His approval from heaven. Following His resurrection, the

Son returned to the throne of His Father, and shortly thereafter the Father sent the Holy Spirit to us earthlings as Comforter and Counselor. And all the time the Three are One!

Oops, I fear I suffer from borderline theologia!

Praise the Lord, I don't have to understand it totally to believe it or to experience it! Matter of fact, the application of the truth of the Trinity is far more precious to me because it demands *faith* of me.

Jesus taught and lived theology constantly. His methods and words were very simple, yet great minds are still trying to probe them, determined to uncover hidden psychological implication or to extricate from them a system of humanistic godship. Maybe Jesus just meant what He said as He said it!

One thing He left no doubt about was that there was a special relationship and purpose between Him and the Father. Jesus put a high premium not only on that relationship but also on their combined objective. In one instance, Jesus indicated that to do the will of the Father was sufficient to feed Him physically as well as spiritually.

John, chapter 4, records Christ's redeeming encounter with the woman at the well—a long encounter! I've always felt an identification with the disciples at this point! Just as they did when it became lunchtime, I would have said, "Let's go eat!" (Preferably something sweet?) Shame on me, for Jesus taught at that well that the hunger of the human heart is infinitely more important than the hunger of the body. And we should give soul hunger first consideration, too.

I believe rebuke was not His intent, however, when He answered the disciples upon their return with "I have meat to eat that ye know not of" (v. 32). No one had fixed

57

Him a sandwich. He had chosen from an unseen menu. "My meat is to do the will of him that sent me, and to finish his work" (v. 34).

How we humans wring our hands over knowing the will of the Father. There is a certain uncertainty about it, too. We can learn a lot of guidelines, though, such as the importance of waiting when uncertain, cross-checking our impulses with the Scriptures, requesting and welcoming the checks of the Holy Spirit, and not *ever* forcing the opening of a closed door.

Add to those principles the fact that His will never houses anything contradictory to His Word. That fact is of the "industrial strength" variety. The foolishness of supposing God has directed or approved our doing something forbidden in His Word is foolishness of Satan's making. I'm not talking about consequences thrust upon us by another's sinfulness or stubbornness, but rather our *selfish rationalization* of God's truth that initiates improper decisions.

Actually, the *stated* will of God as found in His Word makes a surprisingly short list. I refer to those verses that specifically say, "This is the will of God . . ." My search has not been verse by verse as found in book by book, but here are the few I uncovered. They explicitly say that it is the will of God:

> that all should be saved (2 Pet. 3:9)
> that children should be included in redemption (Matt. 18:14)
> that there shall never be loss in the kingdom given to the Son (John 6:39)
> that eternal life shall be the reward to all those who believe on Him (v. 40)
> that all those who are His shall be raised at the last day (vv. 39-40)

that His own (brethren) should be sanctified (1 Thess.
4:3)

From the springboard of His *stated* will we dive head-long into His *implied* will. From there, though, we must be very careful not to swim around pointlessly in the non-sensical pool of the *imagined* will of God.

The implied will of God as contained in the Scriptures is contrasted in its volume to the brevity of His stated will. It is mirrored from Genesis to Revelation. It includes the boundaries of behavior as set by Him. Strictly speaking, His commands are His will. Additionally, the telltale attitudes of His children come from their desire and need to develop a spirit that reeks of divine input. That most surely is His will.

As noted before, man does have the awesome gift of choice. He chooses one side of a two-way street. Nevertheless, God's Word is laden with testimony that He has control over humanity and its destiny and retains for himself the great bulk of decision making. For example, Heb. 2:4 says,

God also testified to it [the message of salvation] by signs, wonders and various miracles, and gifts of the Holy Spirit distributed according to his will *(NIV)*.

Although not stated directly, this confirms that it is the will of God that some should be given various gifts of the Holy Spirit. That is implied. But He reserves unto himself the privilege of selection and distribution.

Let's consider further: Evidently there is an individual plan or will for those who choose to accept Him. We read in Romans this truth:

Do not conform any longer to the pattern of this world, but be transformed by the renewing of your mind. Then you will be able to test and approve what God's will is—his good, pleasing and perfect will *(12:2, NIV)*.

Refuse conformity to the schemes of the world, rejuvenate the thinking by changing the content of the mind, and God will lead you to the discovery of His wonderful and individual will. He *does* have a will for each of us. He writes it in His weekly planner, ready for us when we meet the requirements for revelation.

Furthermore, knowing God's will individually is companion to the process of maturing in the faith. The apostle Paul, drawing his letter to the Colossians to a close, wrote that one of their own, Epaphras, constantly prayed for his fellow parishioners that they, by their understanding of the will of God, might be mature and confident. The King James Version reads, "Perfect and complete in all the will of God" (4:12).

David desired that for himself. His cry was "Teach me to do your will, for you are my God; may your good Spirit lead me on level ground" (Ps. 143:10, NIV).

I have been drawn with interest to a current "big" news story. One of our nation's "stars" has been linked to perverted sexual behavior. At the time of this writing the debate has gone on for days. Just what kind of behavior is off-limits for acknowledged role models? Should the personal life suffer restraints imposed by the public life? Without exception each newscast I heard has allowed someone to parrot: "After all, it's the 80s!" as if society has arrived at a utopian period of freedom that not only allows anything and everything but without doubt nullifies all preexistent guidelines.

What a tragedy that hordes of the youth of our nation will never know the atmosphere of the years long before the 80s when society in general had principles and morals! I realize this is an editorial, but those of us who do not have our heads in the sand or consider it religious prejudice know there *is* an intricate correlation between the mammoth collection of present social ills and the absence of morality and foundational human decency!

I've said that to say this: We in the Church have also found it easy to drift away from some of the earliest hallmarks of Christianity. One of those is the appropriation of the accessible direction of God himself *on an individual basis.* And though this may seem heretical, that includes our own *dilution* of personal moral *liberty or restraint.* Of course, it would be carrying a good thought too far to include the silly definitions of honesty that so many have invented. Besides, it's the 80s!

I grew up hearing my role models exclaim time after time,

"If it's God's will I'll . . ."
"See you tomorrow, God willing."
"We will be there if God wills."
"If God wills I will be working at . . ."
And so on.

I need to admit quickly that just "saying" does not make it so. Nor does it prove we are "doing." Saying "If God wills" should not become a byword of expression with no meaning.

Very early in our marriage Don and I were selling a car. That's not really the way it should be said—Don was selling, I was praying!

One fine Christian man was very interested. "Well," he said, "I love the car. I'll pray about it. If it's the Lord's will I'll buy it."

Sounded good to us. We were mentally spending the money.

A few days later, however, he called to say, "Nope. It's not God's will."

How dare the Lord?

Maybe it's because of my nostalgia streak that I respond with yearning to James 4:13-15:

> Now listen, you who say, "Today or tomorrow we will go to this or that city, spend a year there, carry on business and make money." Why, you do not even know what will happen tomorrow. What is your life? You are a mist that appears for a little while and then vanishes. Instead, you ought to say, "If it is the Lord's will, we will live and do this or that" (NIV).

Wait a minute, James. It's the 80s! Our advanced state provides us the smarts to guide God so He will know what is best for us!

There is a point to be made here concerning the prayer life. Do we realize that God has the power and resource to give us *everything* we ever ask for? Like the ability of wealthy parents, God can give *anything* to us! We believe that, or our asking would be a mockery. It is not God's *ability* that determines whether our requests are granted. Rather, in reality, we are asking for the operation of His knowledge of what is best for us at any given time. He wants us to ask, but He also wants us to trust His perfect will and judgment. How helpful we wish to be!

All that has just been shared with you has been embedded in the rock of my spiritual foundation for years. Still, there are times when it would be great if God would write His orders across the sky in bold letters. He could hire one of those skywriters or tie a banner on the tail of a plane. I would do His bidding immediately!

Wouldn't it be wonderful if God thundered His powerful voice to us, audibly, with specific instructions? One, two, three! We would respond with great heroics and unhesitantly set out to do the world-changing assignments that would surely bring world recognition and honor along the way.

But who says God speaks with thunder? Who says He even blasts His desires for us into some sort of heavenly megaphone? And who says that the most challenging aspect of God's will is harbored in the "great," or wrapped in martyrdom?

Not I!

Not long ago God sent a special gift. I opened it and found it contained a bottle of insight waiting to be poured out as a sweet scent in my life. Nothing earth-shaking, nothing particularly spiritual, nothing transforming—except to me. And I am not going to boast about the results, except to you.

With ribbon and wrapping gone, I discovered that the will of God for me demanded the development of a sensitivity to His still, small voice. I call it "Pat's Still-Small-Voice Syndrome!"

How does it work?

Let's begin by looking at a couple of facts. Probably no one has to return merchandise more often than I. What an assortment of mismatched twosomes, incomplete whatevers, burned-out thingamajigs, and wrongly sized purchases I have toted back to the seller! Fact No. 2: Probably no one gets more disgusted about the whole thing than I do. I want you to know, however, that I am improving. I am learning to inspect the goods more carefully. And I have finally accepted the reality that just because something *looks* like an extra large does not mean it is not a size 6!

Exchanges that are not straight across the board are deadly. And technology has not eased the strain. Computers exhibit no better accuracy with figures than humans. (Do computers use old math or new?) No matter, there I stood one afternoon insisting to the salesgirl that she and the computer had not given correct exchange value. The computer had very little to say, but she was rude—very rude. I admit I argued longer than necessary over what was really a small amount; but it was the principle, you know! We finally came to terms, and I clutched my package firmly and headed for the escalator, inwardly protesting loudly. "You would think a big company like this could afford better help—at least some who were capable of basic adding and subtracting."

My brow was V-shaped, my steps were quick, and I grasped the handrail on the "up" escalator with indignation.

Suddenly the realization came that I had been wrong in figuring, and the salesgirl had been right. Horrors! My ruffled feathers drooped as if caught in a rainstorm.

The still, small Voice: "Go back and apologize to the young lady."

"I can't," I answered. "My pride is on its way to the exit. Besides, Lord, You know how rude she was. She doesn't deserve an apology!"

The still, small Voice again: "I thought you wanted to know My will in a new, very personal way."

I was speechless. The Lord quoted my own prayer words, and with them the prosecution rested. There was no defense, so at the top of the "up" stair my package and I boarded the "down" one!

I approached the cashier's counter with trepidation. Great—no one else was buying anything! The salesgirl still stood staring. I hoped her face had not frozen.

"Going up the escalator," I began sheepishly, "it became obvious that my figures were wrong. You were right all along about the exchange. I am sorry for the way I acted."

As far as I know she may still be standing at her post, glaring. When I saw her last, she had not said a word or changed her expression.

Back to the escalator. So much for being foolish.

Only a few steps were taken when God blessed me in a "very personal" way! There was no preparation for His outpouring. My feet were so full of joy I nearly missed the first step of the escalator. How grateful I am that it did not happen. I would never have known that Penney's had a moving stair that went all the way up to cloud nine!

Could it be that the cares of life would drown themselves in the overflow of His peace if doing His will became as natural as blinking the eyes? One thing for sure, at least they would be gasping for breath.

The Holy Spirit makes it a habit to reward us when we respond to His still, small voice. Experiencing His "surprises" can be astounding. What fun imagining the outcome! He even performs the miraculous on occasion.

I've always been a stickler for punctuality—well, since being married to Don, that is. It's easy to get uptight when I know I'm going to be late.

One morning, while preparing to drive across our big city to be a luncheon guest at a large women's gathering, I was running (literally) behind. After stopping to answer the phone, I heard a voice that brought a silent groan.

Oh, no, not now, came the thought. I knew the lady had problems—serious ones. I couldn't solve them, and I knew the retelling of them would be lengthy.

I reminded myself how important it would be to my hostess to be on time. I hated the thought of arriving at the head table after everyone else had been seated. I opened my mouth to explain that I just couldn't talk then.

But the still, small Voice interrupted. "Sit down. This child of Mine needs someone to listen—now!"

Down I sat on the edge of the bed and listened.

When I finally walked out the front door, I was not yet late. But all of Denver was spread out in plain view. No two points in our city could be much farther apart than our home and the women's meeting. And, in this case, the freeways were of no advantage whatsoever.

Boldness opened the car door. "OK, Lord, You know I did as You said. Now give me green lights from here to there!"

Talk about a modern-day miracle: I drove the entire route without stopping, sitting down at the head table, on time, in peace!

Peace is the prize (yes, with a *z*) of obedience. And *obedience is the test of sincerity:* tests for which we often have little opportunity to cram. They show up out of the blue sometimes.

Out of the blue one day in line at the supermarket, a lady ahead of me had one of everything in her basket. How that happened I don't know, for I try to be smarter than that. I decided she ran a boardinghouse. Poor thing! It's bad enough to have to shop for all of that, much less to have to cook it, too!

My sympathy was already operational when she suddenly gasped. "I have left my checkbook at home," she despaired.

I had done that once, and my sympathy grew.

"I can't go home and come back!" Her voice spoke in weariness. "I live miles and miles from here. I work all week, and I've just been in this area visiting and decided to do my shopping here because the store seemed less crowded than the one I am used to."

She had no need for tears; her *voice* cried.

The Lord spoke: "I want you to pay for her groceries!"

(I know you will laugh but I'm going to tell you anyway: I asked the Lord if He knew what the price of groceries was these days!)

About the time it was evident the Lord was serious, the lady remembered she had some cash. Great! I was off the hook. Just the *big* hook as it turned out. She was still $14.35 short. Again the still, small Voice insisted I pay it.

"Let me pay the balance for you," I said to my anonymous friend.

She was surprised, the checker was surprised, and I was surprised!

I finished the checkout process, hers and mine, and headed for the car. I looked at the detergent and whispered into the air, "What have I done?" The detergent didn't answer, but you-know-who did! "You've done what I told you to do."

No use to remind the Lord that it was, after all, *fourteen dollars and thirty-five cents!* But I did, several times during the next two weeks. During that waiting period my "output" grew to an outrageous sum: fourteen *hundred* and thirty-five *dollars!*

Satan was having fun with this. His approach was to remind me how foolish I had been, that no one did those kinds of things anymore, and that everyone is out for all they can get. The woman probably faked the whole scene. I should have known that the name and address given to the donee would end up in the wastebasket.

"Oh, well," I consoled myself, "at least I showed a couple of people the milk of human kindness." I patted myself on the back with words—easier than twisting my elbow—and chalked up $14.35 to experience.

What surprises were in store! The first one was not that the mail brought a very apologetic letter (the address had been misplaced) accompanied with a check. The check lost its significance when I noted that the letter had been written on scripture stationery! The mystery lady was a Christian! Humiliation crept slowly through my head and heart. God had simply used me to rescue another one of His children from a great inconvenience!

I stood embarrassed before the Lord. Trying to rationalize my stingy attitude, I said, "Lord, it *was* $14.35. A lot of money!"

The second surprise sent me mentally to my knees. The still, small Voice was very tender: "Pat, it was the price of obedience. Was it worth it?"

There was no time to answer. The peace that flooded my being was worth $14 billion and 35 years of experience!

It is the will of the Lord that we learn our lessons well. It is also His will that we rise from our humanness to experience the healing properties of His peace. *His will is not oblivious to green pastures and still waters!*

His will leads us sometimes from crisis to crisis, sometimes through familiar territory with its accompanying comfort, sometimes into uncertain surroundings, and sometimes from valley to mountaintop, and vice versa. And though we much prefer the mountaintop, the Christian not only must be willing to tread the valley, but also asks and believes for God's wisdom for life at any given time. The peace on this level is unequaled.

Sure, the beauty of the valley is best appreciated from the hilltop. But there is no guarantee that the will of the

Father shall station us on a pinnacle. There is no sure promise that His will shall allow us to trace the steps of prosperity. There is no assurance that His will might not involve more of the valley than seems reasonable. But there *is* guarantee, and promise, and assurance (all in great supply) that obedience to the will of our wonderful Lord will produce an exhilarating and stabilizing peace. Even and also when His ways and directions for us are mysterious and uncharted.

Jesus knew it! He guarded His oneness with His Father until at last He knelt among the olive trees and reaffirmed His commitment to the driving impetus of His life: "Not my will, but thine, be done" (Luke 22:42). He rose to face the valley of destiny armed with a meek spirit and abiding peace. Strange—it is past understanding!

4

His Peace Was Sustained by the Presence of the Holy Spirit

The first time I boarded an airplane I felt like a condemned woman. Try as I might, I have not managed to shed that foreboding entirely. Not one molecule of me identifies with the likes of Amelia Earhart! Some of the sweetest words I ever hear come from various airline pilots: "Flight attendant, prepare the door for arrival." The thought comes, Oh, goody, I get to get out!

I have come a long way, however. At least I have perfected the "carriage" of a seasoned traveler, now being able to board a plane and be seated without anyone suspecting I'm about to jump out of my skin.

On one recent flight, though, I almost reverted back to my presophistication days. Just as I took my seat, I noticed how shabby and old the plane was. This piece of carpeted mesh would never get off the ground!

Slowly we hobbled down the runway. Everything on board popped, creaked, spit, banged, and clanged. As we began to gain speed, I was a little under the "whether"! I wondered gravely whether these nuts and bolts would actually get us airborne, whether the pilot was as old as the plane (Orville Wright, maybe?), whether the wings were drooping, and whether anyone else on board knew that we were about to crash! I closed my eyes.

Wonder of wonders, we said good-bye to the ground. Just then a small boy in the row behind spoke gleefully.

"Mommy, are we above the sky yet?"

A foolish, trusting child. Trusting because he did not comprehend danger; foolish because in his childishness he could not fathom the limitless expanse of the sky. Dimensions to him were nebulous. The sky was a "thing" definable by boundaries.

A smile crossed my face. With eyes still closed, I began to reflect on the Holy Spirit. He, too, has no boundaries. He is not limited to spaces, say, 100' by 80'. His work is as the sky, spread over the earth, infinite in its scope. He, too, is a vehicle. It is by His power that man soars to spiritual heights; with full throttle He thrusts wide the door of truth, allowing us to launch into the unsearchable riches of Christ. And though my craft may, at times, be creaky and rusty, He enables me to fly nevertheless!

My meditation pondered the thought that in our zeal to proclaim Christ as King and Messiah and Redeemer, we have minimized the Holy Spirit and His work. I'm sure it has been unintentional. It has had to be, for if we ferret from the Scriptures a description of His work, we are awed.

I can't believe all the Bible says the Holy Spirit will do. What a job description!

One of the best-known declarations is from the lips of Jesus himself: "The Holy Spirit . . . will teach you all things" (John 14:26, NIV).

All things! The whys and wherefores. So He is the One I should ask, and I have to acknowledge His existence and presence to ask Him. What a magnificent, patient personage He is!

In addition to His teaching us, look at all this:

His power strengthens the inner man (Eph. 3:16).
Physical strength is beside the point.

His presence gives hope that overflows (Rom. 15:13).
Hope is the backbone of Christianity.

His control over our minds produces life and peace (Rom. 8:6).
The intellect given to the Spirit of truth (as the Bible calls Him) is energized!

He is the Agent for destroying the misdeeds of the body (Rom. 8:13).
Man needs a discriminator of good and evil.

He witnesses to the world that Christ is an adequate Advocate, sufficient to keep that entrusted to Him (Heb. 10:13-17).
It is ours to tell, His to convince!

He is a translator, conveying to the Father our faltering petitions and immature approaches (Rom. 8:26).
He speaks more than English!

He speaks directly to God's children (Acts 13:2; Rom. 8:14).
He is not a foreign correspondent.

He guides us step by step (Rom. 8:14; John 16:13).
The road signs were created with His counsel.

And that is just the tip of the iceberg!

With all that at our disposal we should be filled with confidence. The Holy Spirit and His operation among mankind is so powerful, so all-encompassing, yet so personal, that when He abides in the human heart, *peace abounds.*

Earlier in this book I have referred to Dr. Corlett's book, *Holiness in Practical Living.* It was written years ago and is of the "oldie-but-goodie" variety. I want to quote him again:

> While many have misunderstood the meaning of this power [the Holy Spirit] and have brought reproach and shame to the cause of holiness by foolish acts and statements, yet this is the true promise of the Father for His children of every generation. It is not sensational power merely to attract and please a curious crowd, but it is primarily power to control man's spirit and to direct his life and service in channels of usefulness in the kingdom of God. It is an establishing power, which is seen in the disciples and apostles through the various persecutions that were brought to them in the record of the book of Acts. It is power to keep poise and character and to manifest a sweet spirit regardless of what others may do. It is the power of a hidden joy that gives happiness in the midst of all kinds of circumstances, whether they be pleasant or unpleasant. Someone misunderstood this to be ecstasy, but ecstasy is simply an outward exhibition of inner enjoyment. There are times when it is not proper and fitting to display ecstasy, but there never is a time when the steady flow of the power of joy is not needed and is not present. It is a power to believe God when everything about would say that God's plan is impossible.

Later, in the same book, these words are found:

> The promise of Pentecost is that the child of God will have power "after that the Holy Ghost is come upon you" (Acts 1:8). This is not the promise of power to be sensational nor abnormal but rather the assurance of power to

keep the fruit of the Spirit manifested in the heart and life of the Christian. It means the removal by the Holy Spirit of the antagonistic nature to God and His will and the perfecting of the heart in divine love. This gives peace of soul, rest of heart, calmness of spirit, and poise of personality!

No wonder Jesus was victorious! Oh, I know in the sense that we date the coming of the Holy Spirit with the Day of Pentecost, the Holy Spirit had not come when Jesus walked the earth. But Jesus had the Holy Spirit! Beside the fact that Jesus was the embodiment of the Trinity, the Holy Spirit came to Him in the form of a dove. We may ask why, if Jesus was already divine, the Father deemed it necessary to send the Holy Spirit to Him and to tell us about it in His Word. Could it be that God was making a statement that if Jesus needed the Holy Spirit in His earthly journey to be victorious and conquering, we dare not suppose we can make it without the Third Person of the Trinity?

Just maybe one of the best-kept secrets in Scripture is the *second* phrase of John 14:26. In the same breath that He declared the Holy Spirit would teach us all things, Jesus said the Holy Spirit "will remind you of everything I have said to you" (NIV).

The words of Jesus were certainly not for one generation or audience. They are for all time and all listeners. When He ascended He left a legacy of unequaled rhetoric with no intention that it would ever be forgotten. Fully aware of man's bent toward forgetfulness and neglect, He and the Father assigned to the Holy Spirit the task of reminding us of just what the Master had said.

And just what did He say? Well, of course, to be totally comprehensive here is not feasible. But, for starters, Jesus repeatedly spoke of repentance, confession, attitudes, Christian behavior reflecting divine love, the new birth, one-on-one relationships, rewards, punishments, life after death, His Father, persecution, His own return to earth, and—where does one stop?

We stop only when we exhaust life itself. There is absolutely no posture of life outside the range of Jesus' words; and the Bible proclaims that the Holy Spirit will remind us of all the promises, the encouragements, the insights, and the truths we shall ever need!

Enjoy with me for a moment:

When there is sin, the Holy Spirit reminds us that Jesus said, "The Son of Man has authority on earth to forgive sins" (Matt. 9:6, NIV).

When there is need, the Holy Spirit reminds us that Jesus said, "Your Father knows what you need before you ask him," and "Ask and it will be given to you . . . for everyone who asks receives" (Matt. 6:8; Luke 11:9-10, NIV).

When there is weariness, the Holy Spirit reminds us that Jesus said, "Come to me, all you who are weary and burdened, and I will give you rest" (Matt. 11:28, NIV).

When there is confusion and deliberation, the Holy Spirit brings to mind that Jesus said, "I am the way and the truth and the life. No one comes to the Father except through me" (John 14:6, NIV).

When there is sorrow, the Holy Spirit reminds us that Jesus said, "I will not leave you comfortless" (John 14:18).

Where there is misunderstanding and criticism, the Holy Spirit reminds us that Jesus said, "Blessed are you when people insult you, persecute you and falsely say all kinds of evil against you because of me. Rejoice and be glad, because great is your reward in heaven" (Matt. 5:11-12, NIV).

When stress and frustration want to overtake us, the Holy Spirit reminds us that Jesus said, "My peace I give you" (John 14:27, NIV).

Needless to say, that list could go on ad infinitum!

What I wish for us to see in those few examples is the glorious fusion of the work of Christ and the work of the Holy Spirit. For it is the *words of Jesus,* brought to us in remembrance by the Holy Spirit, that *mold and condition* our conduct, in turn enabling the Holy Spirit to develop the *fruit* in us that is the *core* of the Christian experience: "Love, joy, peace, patience, kindness, goodness, faithfulness, gentleness and self-control" (Gal. 5:22-23, NIV).

> So I say, live by the Spirit, and you will not gratify the desires of the sinful nature. For the sinful nature desires what is contrary to the Spirit, and the Spirit what is contrary to the sinful nature. . . . Since we live by the Spirit, let us keep in step with the Spirit *(Gal. 5:16-17, 25, NIV).*

Talking about the Spirit is easy. It's the livin' that gets sticky!

What does it mean to be in step with the Spirit? As we all know, steps are the units of progression in walking; therefore to keep in step with the Spirit requires a willing disposition to progress, one pace at a time, with the Spirit as He walks a chosen path. I like the idea of walking side by side with Him. *Following* someone eliminates a great deal of individual thinking, while *side by side* offers great intimacy, freer communication, and warm camaraderie.

Walking implies a universal ability, commonplace and ordinary though it may be. We walk through life. We speak of a daily walk. Why? Because walking is our natural speed of activity. Running and crawling are two variations of transportation, but they are not thought of as normal. Running presupposes fright or urgency, and crawling is most associated with childishness or retardation.

Using this same analogy, when we run or crawl we sometimes forsake the Spirit's presence and pay the consequences of misjudgment. Wouldn't you agree that getting ahead of the Spirit or lagging behind Him is responsible for those stagnant periods in our spiritual maturing that we would just as soon forget?

God would have us walk with the Spirit. That means to keep in step as He leads us through the nitty-gritty, sometimes monotonous, rotation of the weeks. Therein lies success.

Have you read Phillip Keller's *A Shepherd Looks at Psalm 23*? It is difficult to decide which chapter is my favorite. Perhaps it is number 10, which once again reminds us that "He anointeth my head with oil."

I grew up hearing the saints of the church speak of the "oil of the Spirit." Not really knowing what that meant, I reserved understanding for a future day when I, too, would be a "saint."

Phillip Keller was, at one time, a professional shepherd. He informs us that Eastern flocks get very nervous in the spring of the year because of the onslaught of hordes of insects. One of these species is referred to as "nose flies" because they prefer to lay their eggs on the soft, cool noses of the animals. These eggs hatch into larvae that work their way up through the nasal passages into the head of the sheep. Can you imagine the resultant irritation and discomfort? Even as the flies gather in the sky, anticipation causes the sheep to be restless, panicky, and desperate. Some have been known to kill themselves beating their heads against immovable objects in an effort to prevent the landing of these insects.

But how blessed to know that the *good* shepherd is ahead of the game. Before the flies can land he painstakingly covers the head and nose of each sheep with a special oil, a mixture of his own making, and the dreaded

.ot land. Gone is the fright, the aggravation, the
.d the irritability. The sheep rest.

' it is clearer what the saints meant. The Holy
.ttches the "skies" of our world and applies the oil
of His .tature to ward off any harm from the threatening
irritation of daily dilemmas and personality quirks we
must deal with. In advance He anoints our heads with oil
and prepares us for relaxation in the midst of possible destruction and/or stumbling that we are incapable of handling on our own.

Since I am not president of a company, do not rub
elbows with the working world, and am not trying to sell
artificial sweetener to a hive of bees, the nitty-gritty of life
for me is summed up in different ways than for some. I
could probably take an earthquake in stride, but the little
things send me sideways on the walls.

Take, for instance, locking myself out of the house or
car, spilling a jar of bacon grease all over the kitchen, having the vacuum bag explode, finding a flat tire when I am
running late, finding a flat tire when I am *not* running late,
discovering a broken zipper while putting on exactly the
right dress for an occasion, facing an unexpected expense
after having figured the budget to the mill, being out of
vanilla just as the cake is to go in the oven, or accidentally
sending a couple of Kleenex through the washing ma-
chine. And when the checkbook doesn't balance, there is
need for a double dose of the oil! Superficial things, yes.
But they comprise a lot of life for a lot of minutes.

How about dealing with the lady who has copied all
my ideas for a banquet, the mother who does not notice or
care that her child just spilled red Kool-Aid on my white
dress, the telephone solicitor who won't take no for an
answer, the *10th* telephone solicitor to call in one evening,

the paperboy who sails every edition past the driveway and sidewalk, or the "friend" who betrays a confidence?

How about those days when praying is laborious, when the mind is so cluttered or weary that even the 23rd psalm doesn't read well, when everything that can go wrong does and God doesn't seem to be aware of it, when someone cheats you on a business deal, when a mate's love grows cold, or when a spouse is unsympathetic to your faith?

How about being out of money, working with hostility, trying to hope through a terminal illness, or hiding one's head and heart because of a wayward, rebellious child?

Say what you will, walking with the Spirit demands a lot of oil.

But let the world say what it will, the Holy Spirit has a great supply! And He has enough for more than one application per person per episode. True, we only pass this way once. Yet some of life's distresses have a way of reappearing along the path or hanging around for what seems an eternity.

Earlier in this book there was reference to the death of Mother. Daddy died instantly one morning with no chance for us to say good-bye. He was a man of great humor, and my last conversation with him was a very funny one on the telephone.

Daddy was a civil service employee, but he carried out his government job on the railroad. To this day when hearing a train, I steel my jaw or clench my fists. It is hard to bear it without him. Just one more time I would love to laugh at one of his stories, or, after one of his practical jokes, see the twinkle in his eye that said, "Have I put one over on you!" My own tears come easily when remember-

. flow of moisture down his cheeks when God
.n.

so many things remind me of Mother. On occa-
l I can't bear it without her either. Just once more
ove to tell her I love her. She relished those words
more than costly gifts. And it hurts when I have an in-
stinctive urge to call her and say, "Mom, I've had a bad day;
make me a batch of fudge!" Or, "Guess what, Mom, Susan
had a baby girl on your birthday!" "Mom, you should see
this dress I bought!" "Can you believe, Mom, God gave me
my dream: I wrote a book!"

As is true of most of us in retrospect, I regret ever
being impatient with either Dad or Mom, and wish I could
cancel all anxious moments they had because of me.

These emotions are familiar to many of you, I'm sure.
What a minister the Holy Spirit is to me when I struggle
with the reality of life without them, and the finality of
"what is done is done, and what is over is over." He anoints
my head with oil, nudges me to let me know He is *there*,
and reminds me of Jesus' words, "My peace I give you."

Thank God for the Trinity. Thank God for humanity.
Thank God they exist for each other. Thank God for the
apostle Paul, who wrote:

> Therefore, since we have been justified through faith,
> we have peace with God through our Lord Jesus Christ,
> through whom we have gained access by faith into this
> grace in which we now stand. And we rejoice in the hope
> of the glory of God. Not only so, but we also rejoice in our
> sufferings, because we know that suffering produces per-
> severance; perseverance, character; and character, hope.
> And hope does not disappoint us, because God has poured
> out his love into our hearts by the Holy Spirit, whom he
> has given us (*Rom. 5:1-5, NIV*).

NOT AS THE WORLD GIVES

This phrase sends me scurrying for some answers. Did Jesus mean that His *method* of giving was not like that of the world, or did He mean that the *gift* He was giving was different? I was delighted to find in my research that both concepts are acceptable; but it is difficult to decide which aspect I like most! Of course, a divine God gives in ways beyond the capability of humanity, and every good and perfect gift from Him is unequaled by any given by mere man; but I don't want to have to decide or prove which is more significant: God's perfect way of giving or His perfect gifts. Both comprise the blessing of receiving.

Right off the bat I was hung up on one obvious, glaring conclusion: Humans give with strings attached. Everyone knows the world gives from ulterior motives and, as with a kite, attaches strings for the purpose of controlling the vessel. Jesus must have meant that He gives with no strings attached. Mmmm . . .

I inherited my "mail" hormones from Mother. The arrival of the mail was as important to her as breathing. When she was at home the highlight of her day was the walk to the mailbox, and Mother read every piece of junk mail as if it had come from a very dear friend. I remember with amusement the times I spent talking her out of sending for a "great bargain" that she was sure had been offered to *her alone* by a considerate, caring company.

It isn't so amusing anymore, for I catch myself doing the very same thing! I look forward to the mail and devour it all. (Do you suppose that comes with "maturity"?)

Just recently I realized how important the mail had become. I was sitting at the table in the kitchen, mentally listing all the things that helped me function with efficiency.

If I were to do a survey, I mused, which household appliance would win the popularity contest? The dishwasher, the garbage disposal, the electric can opener . . . ?

Suddenly I thought of something else.

Let them haul off all the electric stuff, but don't let them touch my mailbox! I will scrub pots and pans by hand, scrape the dishes into a paper bag, or open cans with my teeth if need be; just don't deprive me of my black-box communication!

That same day, at the same table, I studied the day's "loot." There were two very large envelopes stuffed with almost identical material. Upon examination I discovered I was being offered adventures to exotic places never before heard of, the chance to acquire treasures not known to exist, and the opportunity to have a wardrobe rivaling the queens of the world. All mine just by using the small plastic-coated piece of cardboard both companies would be delighted to send to me.

My suspicious mind began looking for the catch. After reading pages of psychological hype about my sterling character and impeccable credit, in tiny, tiny print I discovered the bottom line. Seems I would have to make periodic remittances on my cardboard purchases, and the company would have to add a few shekels for granting the privilege of "joint ownership!" *There is always a bottom line!*

When Jesus said, "Not as the world gives," He gave us the bottom line to the whole 27th verse, maybe to the entire chapter. With it we can rejoice! There is no catch with God. He gives, but He does not couch His gift amid psychological hype or glittering gimmicks and fantasy promises. (Don't say it: I know that some of His hawkers do, but *God does not!*)

And there are no strings attached—whoops! A little voice said, "Wrong. End of analogy. There is no 'free lunch' even spiritually. When God gives, there *are* strings attached!"

> *If we confess* our sins, he is faithful and just and will forgive us our sins and purify us from all unrighteousness *(1 John 1:9, NIV).*

> *If you remain in me and my words remain in you,* ask whatever you wish, and it will be given you *(John 15:7, NIV).*

> He makes them listen to correction and commands them to repent of their evil. *If they obey and serve him,* they will spend the rest of their days in prosperity and their years in contentment. *But if they do not listen,* they will perish by the sword and die without knowledge *(Job 36:10-12, NIV).*

> *Come* to me, all you who are weary and burdened, and I will give you rest. *Take* my yoke upon you and learn from me . . . and you will find rest for your souls *(Matt. 11:28-29, NIV).*

> God . . . gave his one and only Son, that *whoever believes* in him shall not perish *(John 3:16, NIV).*

> So I say to you: *Ask* and it will be given to you; *seek* and you will find; *knock* and the door will be opened to you. For everyone *who asks* receives; he *who seeks* finds; and to him *who knocks,* the door will be opened *(Luke 11:9-10, NIV).*

> Therefore, if you are offering your gift at the altar and there remember that your brother has something against you, leave your gift there in front of the altar. *First go and be reconciled* to your brother; then come and offer your gift *(Matt. 5:23-24, NIV).*

> If anyone would come after me, he must *deny* himself and *take up his cross daily* and *follow* me *(Luke 9:23, NIV).*

> And everyone who has *left* houses or brothers or sisters or father or mother or children or fields for my sake will receive a hundred times as much and will inherit eternal life *(Matt. 19:29, NIV).*

But the premise is that Christ gives in a manner different from the world. So if there are strings attached, or conditions, to spiritual gifts, wherein lies the difference? For one thing, mystery that it is, God's strings are attached not for the purpose of controlling but rather for providing His children with the greatest freedom they can know. As the Body of Christ we readily admit that His truth shall set us free; yet it is only by the attachment of belief and of the appropriation of His truth that the individual spirit is set *free!*

Furthermore, let's make an observation about the world. I have to admit I have known some nonbelievers who have appeared to be very generous people capable of giving gifts strictly out of love with no strings or hope of return. Or so it seemed. That seems to pose an enigma. But not if we remember that in the final analysis all love comes from God, even though the worldling may not concede that admission.

Love (to be love) has its origin in God. But it is maligned and diluted as it progresses through the channels of sinful man and his self-sustaining behavior. Yet in the midst of sin some seem to be able to love and give very sacrificially without a relationship with God. But this kind of love and sacrifice is *inferior.* In the unconverted even sacrifice is self-serving. The world gives always with some degree of self*ish*ness simply because the unregenerate heart is incapable of acting with pure self*less*ness. "Unlike Christ," you say. Exactly.

Ah, but divine love! The ultimate expression of love, upon which His gift of peace is predicated, was, and is, His life. He gave it knowingly and willingly. He said there is no greater love. In other words, His giving springs from the apex of love that stands on a plane higher than any the

84

world can achieve. And the world is impotent when it would attempt to give in this way.

Oh, to be sure, people have died for causes, some by force, some willingly, but for the world to give a life even willingly without divine love necessitates the embracing of some degree of selfishness and/or egomania. People lay down their lives in suicide much of the time because of misguided selfishness. The very best the world can do is to give an *expression* of love; Christ *is* love. And though salvation is *freely given* it is *experienced* only by those who have met the conditions; the acceptance of Jesus, *His very self.*

What else is different in His manner of giving? Well, Jesus, unlike the world, offers His gift *before* and *without* relationship. The world gives because it has found an object of desire appealing to the emotions, the intellect, the physical, or a combination of all three. The world gives in *response* to fellowship or attraction; God's gifts are given ahead of time in order to make it possible to *establish* fellowship. God gave His only begotten Son *so that . . .*

And His offer is forever. James 1:5 says God gives generously without finding fault (NIV). Many in the world give generously when the relationship is blooming and remains intact. But woe is me when the honeymoon of friendship is over and the marriage must be worked on!

Don and I fell out of favor one time with a friend whose beautiful gift to us had been enjoyed and appreciated for several years. We understood more clearly, however, the fragility of human giving when the friend's messenger came to take it back. The honeymoon and marriage were both over! How unlike God. Man may refuse, "give back," and neglect God's gifts, but He gives without finding fault. He will not dangle the goodies before our eyes only to change His mind if we fail to measure up.

Guthrie wrote a wonderful summary:
(1) The world gives conventionally,
    Christ gives sincerely.
(2) The world gives superficially,
    Christ gives substantially.
(3) The world gives partially,
    Christ gives perfectly.
(4) The world gives capriciously,
    Christ gives constantly.
(5) The world gives temporarily,
    Christ gives eternally.

Shame on the world, hurrah for the Lord!

Now as to the actual gift itself. It certainly exceeds the quality of the world's gift of peace.

We read in God's Word and witness in His universe that the world cries, "Peace, peace." And when there is no peace it turns its fickle attention to substitutions of wealth, recognition, exploited love, and shallow pauses of tranquillity.

In name only does the peace of the world bear any similarity to the peace of God. Probably no other word has been on the lips of earth's inhabitants more in recent decades. But the mental and verbal pictures left by those of the world who speak of peace have little or nothing in common with the variety Christ gives.

The world would bequeath a sterile atmosphere devoid of trouble. Peace is equated in terms of harmony, agreement, utopia, and glib salutation. No wonder the Lord says, "Not like mine!" Oh, that the world could believe that real peace is the result of a relationship between man and his God, a gift outside man's ability to give. Chalk up one unique quality of God's peace: It is only His to give.

There are many ways in which God's peace is different, not the least of which is its permanence. It does not decay. It is not changeable by trends or fads, and though it resides in a vessel of clay subject to deterioration, when properly cared for by its recipient it flourishes and deepens. Perhaps it is more understandable with age, but unlike the world's scarce treasures, it does not appreciate with time; it is priceless from the start!

It is priceless because it does not stand alone. His peace is intertwined with all His other gifts. Lo and behold, His gifts come "boxed" with a small box inside a larger box inside a larger box inside . . .

My grandson was approaching his fifth birthday. We were sitting at my kitchen table when he remembered. His face, resting in his hands, lit up.

"Grandma, what are you going to get me for my birthday?"

I tweaked his nose. "If I tell you," I teased, "it wouldn't be a surprise!"

"Oh, you could tell me," he reasoned, "and then I could forget!"

"But you couldn't *do* that." I laughed.

Whereupon he got down from the table, walked to the center of the room, made an imaginary circle, and returned to the table. His hands held his face again, and his expression was one of mock soberness. "Now," he pretended, "what *was* it we were talking about?"

I was so beguiled I almost spilled the secret of his gift. But that would never do, because my surprises are as much fun for me as they are for him. Now, if you don't think God enjoys giving us surprises, don't tell me. Don't ruin my day.

I know the gifts of God are not kept secret; they are listed in His Word and make up a great package deal. But

I also know God delights in surprising us with additional benefits along the way. Delight has to be the word; no one could give so thoroughly without great enjoyment.

I could write pages about my personal surprises from the Lord. For instance, I rejoice at those times the Lord has used a word or action of mine when I knew nothing about it at the time. The Lord has surprised me with a miracle here and there when it was least expected. He has healed me several times of physical affliction: some of His little surprises!

It's unnecessary to say that God speaks all languages. Even with people, some forms of communication are identical the world over.

I was browsing one day in a lovely gift shop, in a lovely hotel, in . . . well . . . sort of lovely Cairo, Egypt. A native salesclerk was the only other person in the shop. It was marvelous. He spoke no English, and I could look at the beautiful pieces of art without the interruption of all those sales-pitch phrases I was used to at home. After much consideration I decided that since this was the beginning of a long trip and only the first looking I had done, I had better put off buying for a while.

"Maybe *later*," I said, not knowing why I spoke out loud.

Startled, I glanced at the young Egyptian. His smile was a gleaming strip of white stretched broadly across a handsome brown oval. Slowly and with deliberation he said each syllable. "Al-eee-gay-tor?"

A look of recognition and understanding passed between us, and we laughed in the same language.

God speaks the language of the longing heart wherever it is found. His gift of peace is needed and available universally. It does not belong to any certain culture, is not indigenous to a geographical area, does not vary in price from place to place, and has as its marketplace every heart of the human race.

That brings us to one little word at the beginning of John 14:27: *my* peace. This gift is based on the integrity of God. While the gifts of the world are based on impure motives, material pleasure and success, emotional gratification, and earthly significance, Christ's peace is offered with a certified lifetime guarantee backed by the absolute trustworthiness and dependability of God; the company's record and performance is superb! He is able to deliver. The world cannot top an almighty God who has proven true to His Word for aeons past and assures the same fidelity for eternity to come. My typewriter gets blessed at this point!

"Not as the world gives," He said. Not in manner, matter, motive, majesty, or magnitude.

Pity the world!

Epilogue

Meanwhile, back at the ranch . . .

It was Sunday. Looking back, what an appropriate day for a reconciliation!

Not that any of us remotely suspected that it would be. On the contrary, we thought we were at the end of the line. Just three days before, Steve and Sue had attempted to share a Thanksgiving turkey and some meaningful communication. That turned out to be a disaster—the communication, I mean; I don't know about the turkey!

I knew that over the months Sue and the Lord had reached some agreement about the future. I was not surprised, then, that early the day after Thanksgiving she had contacted an attorney. She would see him on her way to work Monday morning.

That's tomorrow, I thought. Tomorrow, tomorrow, tomorrow. Maybe repeating it would get it over with.

It was so quiet in our living room. Sunday nights were often spent in reflection, but our thoughts this night did not include the day's services. I glanced at Don. He was in deep thought, too. We did not need to speak words; we knew our minds were traveling the same track. I suppose some would think it strange that we were not praying. We had prayed many times in many ways, but the appropriate mood now seemed to be to rest in the confidence we professed in God's will and work.

I thought of the surprises of the day. None of us had expected Steve to call. We did not know that that day God had reserved a lunch table for three: Steve and a couple of friends who knew about Sue's Monday morning appointment. Casually they had mentioned it. Probably Steve himself was unprepared for the impact that news would have on him. It jolted him. You see, not only did his present condition cut deep across the grain of his basic integrity and real self, but it was not where he wanted to be with any permanence. Praise the Lord for deeply planted seed!

And so it was that he called Sue to suggest another meeting. They agreed to meet with mutual friends (referees, perhaps!) for one last effort at some kind of progress.

I looked at my watch. Just as I counted up that they had now been talking about five hours, our phone rang. Listening to Don's unsteady voice, I knew it was Steve. They talked at length until, at Steve's request, Don handed the phone to me. Our conversation was short.

"Mom, I have prayed my way back to the Lord. He has forgiven me. Can you forgive me?"

"Sure, Steve." What else could a Christian say?

I reached to return the phone to its cradle, stunned to hear myself thinking, "I don't know whether I can or not!"

This was a foreign battle for me. All my life I had enjoyed the ability to forgive easily, at least until now. And I had bragged to myself along the way about how objective I had been through this experience. I had told myself, and others, that nothing is ever completely one-sided, that I knew Sue had to assume some responsibility, and that "mother-in-law" Pat was not going to allow herself to blame Steve!

On the other hand I had heard my daughter cry herself to sleep, had watched her leave many Sunday nights after church to drive the streets alone until drowsiness would bring her home, had seen the veiled look of disappointment in her eyes. Watching the dissolution of dreams takes it toll. Mothers are like sponges, never ceasing to dry tears or to absorb their wetness. I wasn't so sure about forgiveness after all.

The chair I sat in ceased to be comfortable. I went to bed. When did it get so lumpy?

The sun and I opened our eyes about the same time. It needed no assistance in rising, but I needed a cup of coffee. Don propped the pillows as I prepared the brew. I noticed that he, too, welcomed the caffeine.

The sound of the key in the door stiffened me. I felt a sudden rush of panic. We hadn't seen Steve for months, and frankly I wasn't anxious to then. I said a quick prayer.

How good, good, good God is! It happened so fast. Steve walked through the door, reached his open arms to me, my arms found his neck, and God *obliterated* the past! Forgiveness came as quickly as the water had become wine, as surely as strength had returned to the lame legs, and there remained enough love to fill 12 baskets. In that tick of the clock God taught me one of the cardinal principles of His peace: *It is only feasible when there is forgiveness!* **Simply, and without exception, there is no peace without forgiveness.**

Jesus had so much to forgive. Right! He did it with such ease. Wrong! If Jesus was tempted in all points as we are, He struggled with forgiveness. Had He faltered, there would be no peace for us. Forgiveness is the river through which flows righteousness and rest. *It is the corridor leading the way to divine love.* It is an indispensable brick in the foundation of spiritual growth and survival. Without it, life crumbles.

Do you know how plainly God talks about forgiveness?

And be ye kind one to another, tenderhearted, forgiving one another, even as God for Christ's sake hath forgiven you *(Eph. 4:32).*

And when ye stand praying, forgive, if ye have aught against any: that your Father also which is in heaven may forgive you your trespasses. But if ye do not forgive, neither will your Father which is in heaven forgive your trespasses *(Mark 11:25-26).*

"Lord, don't You want to leave a few loopholes? Surely You meant to insert some 'ifs'? Don't You want to consider the 'extenuating circumstances'?"

Someone has taught the Lord to say, "Nope!"

There are at least three conditions of unforgiveness: the grudge that many hold against God himself; the resentment held for being wronged by another person; and the disposition of self-hate because of personal mistakes. It would be hard to rate them as to which causes the most difficulty. Dealing with any of the three takes discipline and a great deal of soul-searching with God.

In reality it is impossible to forgive God, because man has *no* basis for blaming Him! But the unredeemed man must have a scapegoat, and when he finds himself surrounded by a "fence without a gate," or frustrated by a heartache without explanation, God becomes a convenient dartboard: the target for all the "whys" of life. We may ask, "Why?" forever, but God will not be blamed. He will, instead, lead us to answers. To the grieved heart they may not seem to be definitive, but they will be bearable if God is allowed an inch of acceptance.

Unforgiveness is the forerunner of bitterness, especially when there are other people involved who may or may not be able to right the perception an unforgiving person has developed. What devastation engulfs that individual who simply cannot forgive. I have seen this monster eat away at victims until family, job, and even health are all lost.

Be careful about the process of resolving an unforgiving heart. Forgiving another is first of all between you and God. God will not be pleased to have someone else destroyed by your confession. Restitution is a valid basic of spiritual peace; but it must be God-directed and accomplished with extreme sensitivity when the possibility of personal injury to another exists.

Forgiving oneself may be the toughest of all. The pill of regret is very difficult to swallow. Withdrawal from society, the internalization of blame that blossoms into self-pity, and suppressed anger can all be symptoms that a person cannot forgive his own responsibility in his own misfortunes.

None of us can get away from ourselves. But none of us escapes life without failure and disappointment in our own decisions. Healing begins the moment we deliberately open our heart to an understanding God who is anxious to tell us of our worth. *He* knows us as we are. Self-forgiveness may take awhile, not because of God's limitation, but because clinging tenaciously to self-incrimination is a crutch not easily discarded.

Forgiveness is never impossible or out of reach. That's because Christ is the supreme example. He conquered grudge holding and "I hope they get theirs!" He has forgiven much in that He has suffered much—all unjustly. His suffering at the hands of those who had no right or reason to take His life elevated Him to the throne of God, where He not only sits without malice but intercedes for us that we, too, may be forgiven. It is as the mistreated Redeemer that He has the power to reach into the human heart and replace unforgiveness with serenity, a clear conscience, and yes, even love. His experience provides the grit we need to transform our negative emotions into positive actions.

But we must be willing and vulnerable. And He will not accept a sham, shallow in its dimension or frothy in its words. Forgiveness must be genuine to be acceptable. It must be thorough to be purgative.

God says He will forgive and forget. I know we can forgive. I'm not sure about the forgetting. Yes, I am. We cannot forget. We must not let Satan stick out his foot and trip us with the foolish notion that the inability to forget proves we have not forgiven! The myriad facts and experiences we store in the subconscious are always capable of resurfacing, and may be recalled at any time—triggered into the conscious, sometimes by the most unlikely signal or happenstance.

We know we have forgiven when the remembrance evokes no impulse to action. Our minds may rerun the tape, but when there has been genuine forgiveness there is no desire to hurt another. We may feel sorrow, regret, pain, or even humiliation, but God can deal with unpleasantness and injury until even those remembrances drawn from the subconscious can bring a smile and even warm the heart because of the overcoming peace abiding in their place.

Not all of life's heartaches have the happy ending ours has had. Forgiveness for some is still tied to unchanged circumstances. Sometimes life gets worse rather than better; some people never fall on their knees; sometimes doing everything in our power is not enough. We do not have to wait until the path is flower strewn, or until conditions have righted themselves to our liking to seek out and cultivate a forgiving spirit. Somewhere we *must* find it in ourselves to forgive regardless of our fellowman, in spite of misunderstanding, above personal hurt and sacrifice.

Recognition of an unforgiving spirit is the starting point. Next comes an identification with Christ's own words: "Father, forgive them" (Luke 23:34). That prayer is worthy of hours of repetition if need be. Down that road we hit the pay dirt of peace!

Forgiving, forgiven! These two actions must be operational in our lives. They are as related as inhaling and exhaling. Any significant contribution to God's kingdom will embrace them both. By forgiving I am forgiven. I am forgiven, therefore I dare not fail to forgive!

Dr. William Barclay wrote:

> The peace which Jesus offers us is the peace of conquest. It is the peace which no experience in life can ever take from us. It is the peace which no sorrow, no danger, no suffering can make less. It is the peace which is independent of outward circumstances.

My prayer for you who read is that this peace of God shall be as real to you as flesh and blood, and as daily as the revolutions of the earth, and as sweet as a basket of Easter candies.

How grateful I am to Steve and Sue for allowing me to share with you their part in my search. On second thought, I think I'll call them and thank them personally. They may not have time to read my book; they are *so busy* these days teaching two beautiful little girls that the truths and promises of God are things upon which YOU CAN BET THE RANCH!